TALKING OF GOD

TALKING OF GOD

An Introduction to Philosophical Analysis of Religious Language

by
Terrence W. Tilley

PAULIST PRESS
New York/Ramsey/Toronto

Library of Congress
Catalog Card Number: 78-51592

ISBN: 0-8091-2110-7

Published by Paulist Press
Editorial Office: 1865 Broadway, New York, N.Y. 10023
Business Office: 545 Island Road, Ramsey, N.J. 07446

Printed and bound in the
United States of America

Preface

Many Christian believers and thinkers are convinced that empirical philosophy only attacks religious faith. *Talking of God* shows that such a conviction is a misplaced half-truth. Empiricism has taken a variety of paths beyond the verificationism of the 1920's and 1930's and the falsificationism of the 1950's. Most empiricists not only acknowledge the meaningfulness of religious belief, but attempt to understand the truth(s) found therein. Many empiricists have attempted to show how believers—and their opponents—can understand, clarify and justify their basic religious—or anti-religious—beliefs. While empiricism may not be a comfortable handmaid to theology, critical philosophy is not necessarily antithetical to religious faith.

I write as a Catholic and an empiricist to show how analytical-empirical philosophy can be of use in understanding faith. Many critics, from tough-minded logical positivists to soft-hearted Christians, have helped me along the way. Chief among them are David Rynin and James McClendon, whose incisive criticisms of early drafts of parts of the first four chapters brought clarity to the text; William C. McFadden, S.J., whose reading of the final typescript culled out numerous infelicities; John F. Haught, whose proofreading corrected many blunders; and Maureen Tilley, who read, corrected and fought with me lovingly over every part of the text at every stage. To these—and to all the inspiring teachers, encouraging colleagues, scintillating students, faithful friends and suffering relatives who have helped improve this book immeasurably—thanks!

Terrence W. Tilley
Washington, D.C.
January 1978

Contents

Introduction

The beginning of the twentieth century marked the emergence of a new vitality in empirical philosophy. Empiricists are those philosophers who subscribe to the notion that all knowledge begins in experience. Whether they are commonsense philosophers like G. E. Moore, logical atomists like Bertrand Russell, radical empiricists like William James, logical positivists like A. J. Ayer or ordinary language analysts like John L. Austin, all would agree that human experience is the ground or source of human knowledge.

Most empiricists have been rather hostile to religious faith. In the eighteenth century, John Locke, the "father" of empiricism, was a strong Christian and a staunch defender of religious toleration, yet his famous "son," David Hume, was notoriously agnostic (though notably genial and moral). All of the above-mentioned twentieth-century empiricists, save James, either had little to say on religious beliefs or were actively anti-religious. However, this sort of hostility has been diminishing as empirical philosophy has become more tolerant of and more interested in religious faith.

The distinguishing mark of much of twentieth-century empiricism has been its concern with language. The Austrian-born genius Ludwig Wittgenstein was most influential in this regard. Wittgenstein, in both his writing and his teaching, showed that understanding the language we use is at least the first step in understanding the world in which we use it. Many of the techniques used in empirical philosophy today owe their first use or inspiration to Wittgenstein.

Attempting to understand language as it is (rather than as it "should be" according to some pristine standard) has led some people to attempt to understand religious language and give an account of the language religious people use. In the last thirty years, numerous accounts of "God-talk" have been developed,

1

most of them concentrating on the form or logic of religious language. Rather than being chary of talk of God, many empirical philosophers are again approaching this as a genuine and interesting philosophical problem or task.

The purpose of this book is to examine some classical and modern theories of talk of God, with special reference to the problems of the sense of this talk and of its reference. By "sense" I mean what we would call "meaning." One knows the sense of a concept or utterance if one knows how to use it. By "reference" I mean "naming." If a concept or utterance points to, or names, some object (or objective), it is said to refer. The use or meaning of an utterance or concept can be discovered apart from questions concerning whether it actually refers to what it supposedly refers to and whether there is anything to be referred to. For instance, we can all understand how to talk about Santa Claus and can be said to know the meaning of the concept "Santa Claus"; we all know how to use sentences with the words "Santa Claus" in them and can be said to know the meaning of those sentences or utterances. But do these sentences point to, name or refer to any being? Or, to put it differently, is there a real person named Santa Claus about whom we speak when we use the words "Santa Claus"? Most adults would claim that there is no such person; he is a "legend" or a "myth" or an "imaginary personification of the Christmas spirit." Yet even those adults who don't believe in Santa still can read "Twas the night before Christmas . . ." with some pleasure and do read the tale to their children. It does not matter that Santa stories are not "true to the facts"; they have more important work to do, e.g., teaching generosity. The point is that one can still talk *meaningfully* of Santa without *referring* to some person or object, without believing that a "real" person exists about whom such talk must be if it is to be meaningful. In general, our talk can be meaningful and make sense whether or not it refers, whether or not it is about something "real."

There are those who claim that something similar can be said about talk of God; it does make sense although there is no real person, being or objective to which "God" refers. The second chapter deals with some theories of talk of God that take this position. Talk of God is meaningful, but it does not refer. These theories seem to be an improvement on the claims of the narrow empiricists presented in chapter one who claim that talk of God is nonsense! The third chapter details some theories holding that, not only is there some sense to talking of God, but also such talk does refer to God. The fourth chapter then presents a pair of theories that give a comprehensive account of the sense of talk of God, and discover a referent for that talk. The final chapter explores the ways in which talk of God is to be justified. Perhaps the most important debate today among theorists of religious language is whether or not talk of God can be justified.

Having mentioned the background against which this book situates itself and having outlined its content and structure, let me say what it is not. It is not a final word, but a first step. It does not settle a debate, but invites you to enter into an ongoing discussion. It is not a technical contribution to that discussion but a critical introduction to the main issues of the discussion. It is not going to teach you a new jargon, for it avoids jargon whenever possible, but not at the expense of precision. For better or worse, *some* precise shorthand terms are necessary to facilitate the discussion.

Theologians have been as wary of empirical philosophy as empiricists have been of religious faith. But not only has the scope of empiricism been growing, theologians have also begun to see that analytical-empirical philosophy can make a contribution to the understanding of religious faith. What this book hopes to show is how the renewed vigor of empiricism that began at the turn of the century and continues today can contribute to a new vitality in theology as we approach the end of the twentieth century.

1
Narrow Empiricists

Throughout the course of human history, people have talked of God and the gods. For the most part, it has been taken for granted that talking of God has made sense. For the most part, people have believed that there were gods or a God for them to refer to when they were talking. However, these assumptions have been challenged. One of the clearest challenges was issued by British empiricist philosopher David Hume (1711-1776) who denied that talk of God made any sense—and since it made no sense, it could not point at or refer to any gods or god.

David Hume

Perhaps the classic statement opposing rational belief in and talk of God is contained in Hume's *Inquiry Concerning Human Understanding*:

> If we take in our hand any volume of divinity or school metaphysics, for instance; let us ask, *Does it contain any abstract reasoning concerning quantity or number?* No. *Does it contain any experimental reasoning concerning matter of fact and existence?* No. Commit it then to the flames: for it can contain nothing but sophistry and illusion.[1]

Hume considered what he called the "religious hypothesis" useless, and therefore senseless. Belief in God contributes nothing to our knowledge: "No new fact can ever be inferred from the religious hypothesis . . . beyond what is already known by fact and observation."[2] Hence, preaching belief in God is sophistry and believing in God is illusion.

Moreover, in his *Dialogues Concerning Natural Religion*, published three years after his death, Hume claimed that all argument about God was nonsense, whether one attempted to argue for the existence of God, or against the existence of God, or about what sort of God there is. Hume first demolished the argument from design ("Just as our analysis of a watch we discover lying in a field compels us to infer the existence of a watchmaker, so does our analysis of the Universe compel us to infer a universe-maker or God"). We base our inference of a watchmaker on numerous experiences and analyses of watches, but our inference of a universe-maker is baseless since we can experience and analyze only *one* universe. The analogy between watches (and watchmakers) and universes (and universe-makers) flops since the first part is based on many experiences (and is thus justifiable) while the second is based on only one (and is thus unique and thus the inference is unjustifiable). But even if this objection does not hold, *what* can we infer from the argument? How many gods made the universe? As many or one may make a watch, could many or one make a universe? And how could we decide which was the case? These unanswerable questions destroy the traditional argument to God from the design of the world.

Second, Hume shows the problems with one form of the ontological argument. This argument does not rely on experience, but on logic. But for any argument to be affirmed on the basis of logic alone, any such argument, including the ontological, must not be reasonably dubitable or contradictable. That is, it must demonstrate a necessary truth (one that cannot be reasonably doubted, or doubted without self-contradiction; e.g., if one doubts that all widows are women, one is involved in a self-contradiction) to be successful; and "God exists" is not a necessary truth (for it can be doubted without self-contradiction).

Third, Hume presents the problem of evil as a major reason to doubt the existence of God as he is traditionally conceived. His statement of the problem is a classic:

Epicurus's old questions are yet unanswered. Is he willing to prevent evil, but not able? then is he impotent. Is he able, but not willing? then is he malevolent. Is he both able and willing? whence then is evil?[3]

Talk of God's infinite power, infinite love, infinite mercy, infinite justice and infinite wisdom is, according to Hume, impossible, for his attributes in *no* way seem to resemble these attributes when people have them. If there is not a close analogy between human and divine goodness, then while we may be able to understand what it means to call some person good, it is difficult—Hume would claim impossible—to say what it means to call God good. Emotionally and intellectually the affirmation of the existence of God in the face of perceived evil is problematical.

Finally, in the concluding section of the *Dialogues*, Hume has his protagonist summarize the dispute between the theist and the atheist as follows:

All men of sound reason are disgusted with verbal disputes, which abound so much in philosophical and theological enquiries. . . . That the dispute concerning theism is of this nature, and consequently is merely verbal, or perhaps, if possible, still more incurably ambiguous, will appear upon the slightest enquiry. I ask the theist if he does not allow, that there is a great and immeasurable, because incomprehensible, difference between the *human* and the *divine* mind: The more pious he is, the more readily will he assent to the affirmative, and the more will he be disposed to magnify the difference: He will even assert that the difference is of a nature which cannot be too much magnified. I next turn to the atheist, who, I assert, is only nominally so, and can never possibly be in earnest; and I ask him, whether, from the coherence and apparent sympathy in all the parts of this world, there be not a certain degree of analogy among all the operations of nature, in every situation and in every age. . . . He will readily acknowledge it. Having obtained this concession, I push him still farther in his retreat; and I ask him, if it be not probable, that the principle which first arranged, and still maintains, order in this universe, bears not also some

remote, inconceivable analogy to the other operations of
nature, and among the rest to the economy of human mind
and thought. However reluctant, he must give his assent.
Where, then, cry I to both these antagonists, is the subject of
your dispute? The theist allows, that the original intelligence
is very different from human reason: The atheist allows, that
the original principle of order bears some remote analogy to
it. Will you quarrel, Gentlemen, about the degrees and enter
into a controversy, which admits not of any precise meaning,
nor consequently of any determination? If you should be so
obstinate, I should not be surprised to find you insensibly
change sides; while the theist on the one hand exaggerates the
dissimilarity between the supreme Being, and frail, imperfect, variable, fleeting, and mortal creatures; and the atheist
on the other magnifies the analogy among all the operations
of nature, in every period, every situation, and every position. Consider then, where the real point of controversy lies,
and if you cannot lay aside your disputes, endeavour, at least,
to cure yourselves of your animosity.[4]

Those who talk of God differ from those who do not talk of God
only verbally—or so claims David Hume. And if the only difference is verbal, there is no real difference at all. Hume makes this
clear in a note: "The only difference, then . . . is, that the sceptic,
from habit, caprice or inclination, insists most on the difficulties;
the dogmatist, for like reasons, on the necessity [of believing in a
cosmic designer]."[5] In other words, there is not a bit of intellectual
difference between them, and their agreement is hidden by their
differing words, and the argument over the existence of God is
meaningless.

But the question to ask Hume is whether the differences ever
are or can be *merely* verbal? If the differences between the atheist
and the theist are verbal alone, there are no real differences between them. But is it not the case that the verbal differences arise
from more fundamental differences? Is it not the case that differences in beliefs about what is ultimate are not always due to "habit,
caprice or inclination," but may be due to one's interpretation of

the facts that one sees—and may not different interpretations of the facts lead different interpreters to lead rather different lives? In fact, the differences between theist and atheist are rarely verbal alone.

Hume did not have the philosophical tools to analyze those differences that seem to be merely verbal, nor was he able to decide, according to his understanding of experience and knowledge, just which disputes were verbal and which were significant. While Hume's negative arguments are devastating, he leaves us with our feet firmly planted in mid-air, unable to touch down so as to make progress toward the goal of understanding any meaning for talk of God. What we need is a more sophisticated understanding of our language and a clearer account of the differences between theists and atheists. Sir Alfred Julius Ayer more recently denied that talk of God made any sense and thus could have a reference, but did so on the basis of a more sophisticated theory of language. He also discovered at least one difference between atheists and theists.

A. J. Ayer

In a manner reminiscent of Hume, Ayer attempted to refute the claim that religious beliefs could be true or false. It was his position, much like Hume's, that only two types of statements could be held as literally meaningful: tautologies (those that define themselves, such as "A equals A") and those that are empirically verifiable. Those that could not be verified or falsified empirically, such as metaphysical claims, were dubbed "meaningless." Ayer summarized his position on talk of God as follows:

> For to say that "God exists" is to make a metaphysical utterance which cannot be either true or false. And by the same criterion, no sentence which purports to describe the nature of a transcendent god can possess any literal significance . . . all utterances about the nature of God are nonsensical.[6]

Talk of God is not literally significant for it tells us no new fact about the real world. Such talk, having nothing to do with facts, cannot be coherently proposed or opposed. It simply says nothing. At best, religious talk of God may be an expression of one's attitudes or emotions, which tell us nothing of the world beyond the speaker's mind, and certainly not of any god. The claim that a believer would make, that he is indeed talking of a real God, whose reality is as clear to him as the reality of the world, or himself, is denied. Since such a claim cannot be empirically investigated, it must not deal with matters of fact. Since it does not deal with matters of fact, it cannot be true or false. Since it cannot be true or false, it is nonsense. And talk that makes no sense surely cannot refer to anything—for if it makes no sense, we cannot know what it means or whether it actually does refer to something.

Ayer does offer one suggestion for understanding the sense and reference of talk of God:

> It is to be remarked that in cases where deities are identified with natural objects, assertions concerning them may be allowed to be significant. If, for example, a man tells me that the occurrence of thunder is alone both necessary and sufficient to establish the truth of the proposition that Jehovah is angry, I may conclude that, in his usage of words, the sentence "Jehovah is angry" is equivalent to "It is thundering."[7]

But here Ayer simply overplays his hand. If there is an actual equivalence between the two sentences, it would make sense for a person to say "It is thundering" and for another person to respond "Yes, I wonder who Jehovah is angered with." The real oddity of this response suggests that Ayer's necessary and sufficient conditions for the sentence to be meaningful are not adequate. It would be odd for a believer to set up the necessary and sufficient conditions for determining the meaning or truth of the claim in the way Ayer did. The theist's conditions would be somewhat more complex than Ayer's and would not include the rather absurd picture of a human-like form sitting on a cloud hurling lightning bolts and clanging cymbals as a reasonable representation of God. So Ayer's "concession" is, in the end, useless and empty.

However, a more fundamental problem arose in regard to Ayer's philosophical position. This position allowed that only two sorts of language could be meaningful: tautologies and those propositions that are verifiable empirically. Ayer formulated his verification principle as follows:

> The criterion which we use to test the genuineness of apparent statements of fact is the criterion of verifiability. We say that a sentence is factually significant to any given person, if, and only if, he knows how to verify the proposition which it purports to express—that is, if he knows what observations would lead him, under certain conditions, to accept the proposition as being true, or reject it as being false. If, on the other hand, the putative proposition is of such a character that the assumption of its truth, or falsehood, is consistent with any assumption whatsoever concerning the nature of his future experience, then, as far as he is concerned, it is, if not a tautology, a mere pseudo-proposition.[8]

However, how are we to verify the verifiability principle itself? It is certainly not a tautology. Is there any conceivable future experience that is inconsistent with it? Apparently not. Hence, *it* must be a pseudo-proposition or nonsense! And indeed, on Ayer's standards, it seems that the verification principle is as metaphysical as talk of God.

The history of the debates about the verification principle is too extensive to enter into here.[9] However, in standard, correct, ordinary English, there are "facts" other than scientific facts, there are "meanings" other than verifiable meanings, and there are "truths" other than literal truths. And none of these are necessarily nonsense. While theological language may have some meaning other than the communication of scientific facts, that does not imply that such language is nonsense or purely emotive. If talk of God is supposed to be giving a scientific explanation of the way the world is, then it is open to scientific verification. But if such talk attempts to disclose facts beyond those available to science, then scientific verification—or falsification—is not a sufficient test of that language.

Talk of God, according to the ordinary religious speaker, does refer to something not describable in scientific terms, but nonetheless meaningfully affirmable as existent.[10] If our language does other work besides communicating scientific data, then talk of God may legitimately be claimed to be meaningful, and perhaps even to refer successfully to a god. Frederick Ferré has stated the problem acutely:

> That theological discourse has been shown to be untenable when interpreted as pseudo-scientific explanation, does not, it would appear, rule out the possibility of its functioning rationally and legitimately in some other way. Verificational analysis does not recognize any other way, but this may illustrate a shortcoming more in verificational analysis than in theological language.[11]

With that harsh truth, we must leave verificationism to seek a more sympathetic and flexible approach to the problem of accounting for talk of God.

Antony G. N. Flew

Flew, an atheist philosopher informed by a more sympathetic understanding of traditional Christian claims, issued the "Falsification Challenge" in 1950. He asked what could count against the Christian's belief in God: If nothing could possibly count against it, isn't such belief, then, empty—and hence meaningless? Finding that Christians will allow nothing to count against their faith, he claimed that it is not meaningful to believe in God (and thus that such talk cannot refer). Flew's work can be examined under three main topics: (1) his account of the sense of talk of God; (2) his proposal for the method of examining talk of God; (3) the conclusions he comes to about the reference of such talk. Understanding his approach is important, for it is typical of many allegedly neutral approaches to talk of God, which seem reasonable, but are often biased.

First, Flew refuses to allow any analysis of talk of God as emotive, prescriptive or normative. The non-cognitive approaches (considered fully in Chapter 2) forfeit the debate between theists and atheists before it begins. Reacting to R. M. Hare's analysis of talk of God as expressing a fundamental, neither-true-nor-false, presuppositional attitude (Hare calls this a *blik* [a made-up word]), Flew objected:

> I nevertheless want to insist that any attempt to analyse Christian religious assertions as expressions or affirmations of a *blik* rather than as (at least would-be) assertions about the cosmos is fundamentally misguided. First, because thus interpreted they would be entirely unorthodox. If Hare's religion really is a *blik*, involving no cosmological assertions about the nature and activities of a supposed personal creator, then surely he is not a Christian at all?[12]

Flew made this claim more general and more explicit in his later book *God and Philosophy*: ". . . certain philosophers have tried to analyse the meaning of religious utterances in normative, as opposed to descriptive terms. This bizarre enterprise . . . is a mockery of the faith of the saints and the Fathers."[13] While this sounds like only a motive for consideration of theological utterances as descriptive, it is actually a good reason. Flew claimed that inasmuch as analysts of religious language "discover" that talk of God is non-cognitive, they cannot give an adequate account of the way the saints and the Fathers talked. Unlike Ayer, Flew acknowledges that talk of God is possibly true. But like Ayer (and probably Hume), Flew believed that the claims made by believers are false. So a major part of the sense of talk of God is a claim as to the way the world is—a creation of an Infinite Creator.

Another aspect of talk of God is the alleged referential work that such talk does. Most believers, when asked what they were speaking of in talking of God, would answer "A Being which is unique, unitary, incorporeal, infinitely powerful, wise and good, personal but without passions, and the maker and preserver of the Universe."[14] Flew takes this Being as the intended reference of Christian talk of God. Of course, that the reference is *intended* does not mean that there *is* a God for such talk to refer to.

Next, Flew takes the position of an outsider, a neutral philosopher, as the proper vantage point for examining the claims of the theist. "The philosopher of religion," Flew claims, has as such no business to be counsel for either the prosecution or the defense. If any juridical model is apt, it is that of the examining magistrate."[15] Yet Flew believes that the procedure to be followed involves what he calls the "presumption of atheism" which is analogous in theological debate to the presumption of innocence that the accused has in English and American common law.

> What the protagonist of my presumption of atheism wants to show is that the debate about the existence of God ought to be conducted in a particular way, and that the issue should be seen in a certain perspective. His thesis about the onus of proof involves that it is up to the theist: first, to introduce and to defend his proposed concept of God; and, second, to provide sufficient reason for believing that this concept of his does in fact have an application.[16]

Flew claims that the "presumption of atheism" is neutral between atheists and theists and is merely a methodological presumption, not a substantive assumption.

However, Flew's approach to traditional Christian theism reminds one more of the traditional anti-Christian skeptic than of the neutral examining magistrate. As Dallas High has noted in regard to the "Falsification Challenge":

> Flew's insistence on trying to find what could "count against" (and therefore a way of understanding the meaning [of]) "believer-talk" is not as straightforward as it looks. Flew has already rigged the rules of the game for "meaning" and "falsification" . . . a rigging we do not have to grant. That is, he has already determined in advance that "meaning" must entail "falsification."[17]

By making the claims that "all assertion must involve a theoretical possibility of error precisely proportionate to its content"[18] and, following W. K. Clifford, that it is "wrong always, everywhere, and for everyone, to believe anything on insufficient evidence,"[19]

Flew implies that all assertions must necessarily be the expression of hypotheses. Following Hume, he even talks of "the religious hypothesis."[20] But is this not a mistake? Can hypotheses be religious? Can faith in God be hypothetical? Can the language that expresses such faith be the assertion of a hypothesis? Can any ultimate claims be asserted hypothetically? To all of these, the believer answers "No!" And Antony Flew himself can show us why that "no" is justified! In concluding *God and Philosophy*, Flew wrote:

> We therefore conclude, though as always subject to correction by further evidence and further argument, that the universe itself is ultimate; and hence, that whatever science may from time to time hold to be the most fundamental laws of nature must, *equally provisionally*, be taken as the last words in any series of answers to questions as to why things are as they are. The principles of the world lie themselves "inside" the world.[21]

But is there not something rather strange about the "hypotheses" that (1) the universe is ultimate; (2) science has the last word; (3) the principles of the world lie within the world? What evidence could possibly falsify them—what evidence that Flew *would admit into his court* could falsify them? And if Flew is to follow Clifford's principle, what evidence supports the claims he made? If *all* evidence is consistent with these claims, then they are unfalsifiable, and by Flew's standards, meaningless.

Flew has assumed the pose of the neutral scientist or the detached magistrate whose theories or verdicts are subject to correction on the basis of further evidence and argument. However, there is some evidence that Flew would neither admit nor evaluate. In a discussion of "Religious Experience" he argues that it is "impossible to rely for proof upon some supposedly self-authenticating experience."[22] While on the face of it the principle he enunciates is persuasive, two problems arise. First, these "experiences" *may* refer to something. The religious believers' claims to experience God *may* be purely subjective, self-deluding or totally illusory; or they *may* be just what they claim to be. What we need is some way to evaluate these experiences to see if they belong in court, or to discover what weight they are to be given when they are presented. Unhappily, Flew offers no suggestions as to their evaluation. This leads to the second problem, that Flew threw these "evidences" out of court without a clear reason for saying *why* they should be thrown out of court, since he could see no way in which they could fit in his courtroom. This clearly marks Flew not as impartial magistrate, but as prosecuting attorney; not as detached scientist, but partisan scrapper.

With deceiving clarity, Flew has attempted to set up the game of the debate between the believer and the agnostic in such a way that excludes a priori those evidences that the believer finds compelling. And it simply is the case that not all disputes are to be settled by the examining magistrate: Some claims are not satisfactorily adjudicable from the outside. For instance, if I make the claim, "My wife is a great lover," how could one falsify it? From the bench? No, some claims may be decidable on evidence that is available only from the perspective of those *involved*, not from the perspective of those who are neutral. Some claims—and many theists would say this is part of the case with their claims—require an "insider perspective" to judge them properly. And Flew has excluded these sorts of claims from proper evidence.

Flew also practices some deception here, although it is unintentional. He has tried to assume the position of an impartial and neutral judge, when in fact his is the position of the adversary of theism. Flew is quite clearly correct in claiming that believers are making assertions. But the adequacy of those assertions cannot always be judged from an Archimedean platform or a judge's bench. As soon as one argues for or against those assertions or for or against evidence in their favor, one has stepped down from the bench (or reentered the atmosphere) and become either a prosecuting attorney or a defending counsel (or an earthbound human). And Flew has made this move without notifying the reader that he has done so.

Flew finds no evidence for the religious hypothesis. So, although it may make some sense, it certainly cannot in any sense be true, and there cannot be any Being for talk of God to refer to. But it seems that the sense Flew finds for talk of God is rather at odds with that which believers would find to be its sense. While Flew takes seriously the fact that speakers claim talk of God to be true, he ignores the status most speakers would claim for such talk. It is talk that is not only "true" (taken as a scientist may talk about a true hypothesis, which is how Flew takes "true"), but a "more profound truth" that involves not only one's hypothesis-forming intellect but rather the "whole self." Talk of God is not thought to be a scientific law about some occurrences, but a conviction about all there is. Theistic utterances have neither the same grounds, nor supports, nor functions that scientific hypotheses have. While there may be overlap between religious convictions and scientific hypotheses, the assumption that each of these has the same "logic" is simply wrong.

The real crux of the matter is the opposing beliefs among folk who find the world just ordinary and those who find that the ordinary can speak of the extraordinary. Whatever else it may be, talk of God is extraordinary, beyond the range of science. If Flew's three convictions are correct, then talk of God is indeed senseless. But Flew, like Ayer and Hume, offers us no grounds on which to affirm either his or a theist's convictions. The evidence that might help—the experience of the extraordinary in and through the ordinary—is disallowed. But if there are some extraordinary events, events that scientific assertions cannot adequately portray, or if there is depth within our human horizons, then talk of God, in whom we live and move and have our being, is one way to speak of what is extraordinary. Talk of God must then be judged in ways appropriate to all ultimate claims—including Flew's—in a courtroom modeled on a civil, not criminal, case where there is no assumption or presumption favoring either side. Flew's account of the matter—putting theism on trial—is simply the outcome of an unhappy analogy. What is on trial is what we are to believe about the ultimate, and both Flew's and the theist's beliefs are in the dock. Flew thinks that defeating the theist's case is finally sufficient—but what of supporting his own? When all is said and done, Flew's own convictions are as senseless (or sensible) as those of the theist.

If the only facts are scientific facts, if the only meanings are clearly specifiable meanings, if the only truths are literal truths, then a position like those taken by Hume, Ayer and Flew is the proper position. But if the world is richer than the literal, straightforward, and clear language of science says, then another position is needed. The concept of God, expressed in believers' talk of God, does not meet the standards of impersonal scientific language or of flat and uninspiring everyday talk. Nor is talk of God or the ultimate as clear as more prosaic talking.[23] But that does not necessarily make it devoid of sense and totally without reference.

But this leads to the next question: What sense *does* talk of God have? Numerous answers have been given by philosophical theologians, each of which is able to find some positive sense of talk of God. In chapter two we can explore one group of theologians who discover some non-cognitive (i.e., not amenable to evaluation as true or false; having little or nothing to do with the intellect) status for talk of God.

Notes

1. David Hume, *An Inquiry Concerning Human Understanding*, ed. L. A. Selby-Bigge, 2nd ed. (Oxford: Oxford University Press, 1902), XII, p. 164.

2. *Ibid.*, p. 147.

3. David Hume, *Dialogues Concerning Natural Religion*, ed. Norman Kemp Smith, 2nd ed. (London: Thomas Nelson, 1947; New York: Bobbs Merrill. [Library of Liberal Arts], n.d.), p. 198. For the theological response to the problem of evil see John Hick, *Evil and the God of Love* (London: Macmillan, 1966) or Michael Galligan, *God and Evil* (New York: Paulist Press, 1976). Hick's treatment is an exhaustive historical survey and is now available in paperback from Collins. Galligan's treatment is much briefer and concentrates primarily on more recent approaches to the problem.

4. Hume, *Dialogues*, pp. 217-19. This section was part of the final revision Hume made of the *Dialogues* in 1776, the year of his death.

5. *Ibid.*, p. 219.

6. A. J. Ayer, *Language Truth and Logic*, 2nd ed. (New York: Dover Press, 1952), p. 115.

7. *Ibid.*, p. 116.

8. *Ibid.*, p. 35.

9. For an excellent summary of the debate see R. W. Ashby, "Verifiability Principle," *The Encyclopedia of Philosophy*, ed. P. Edwards (New York: Macmillan and Free Press; London: Collier Macmillan, 1967), VIII, pp. 240-47.

10. There are some theologians, e.g., Paul Tillich, who would claim that it is improper to say that God exists. The reasoning is that God is beyond our mundane distinction between essence and existence, so we ought not to say that he exists. The ordinary believer's assertion of the existence of God is not being criticized here. Rather, suggestions are being offered for understanding the proper metaphysical *mode* for God's existence. But before we can argue about the *sort* of existence God has, we must first decide whether there is, in any sense, a God. The ordinary believer usually intends only to affirm that belief, not to make a metaphysical argument.

11. Frederick Ferré, *Language, Logic and God* (New York: Harper and Row, 1969), p. 45.

12. A. G. N. Flew, "Theology and Falsification," in *New Essays in Philosophical Theology*, ed. A. Flew and A. MacIntyre (London: SCM Press, 1955; New York: Macmillan, 1970), pp. 107-8. Cf. A. Flew, " 'Theology and Falsification': Silver Jubilee Review," in *The Presumption of Atheism* (New York: Harper and Row; London: Pemberton Publishing, 1976), pp. 71-80, for Flew's latest thoughts on the "falsification challenge."

13. A. G. N. Flew, *God and Philosophy* (New York: Harcourt, Brace and World, 1966 [reprinted in paperbound form: New York: Dell, n.d.]), pp. 22-23. His argument is directed primarily against the position of R. B. Braithwaite (whom we consider in ch. two) and S. Toulmin.

14. *Ibid.*, p. 28. But is this the *only* Christian sense of the word "God"? Many would argue that to take this *literally* is presumptuous and process theologians would claim to have discovered another, more adequate sense for "God."

15. *Ibid.*, p. 26.

16. Flew, "The Presumption of Atheism," in *The Presumption of Atheism*, p. 15.

17. Dallas M. High, *Language, Persons and Beliefs* (New York: Oxford University Press, 1967), p. 151.

18. Flew, *God and Philosophy*, p. 133.

19. Flew, "The Principle of Agnosticism," in *The Presumption of Atheism*, p. 32.

20. Flew, *God and Philosophy*, p. 194. Cf. "The Religious Hypothesis," in *The Presumption of Atheism*, pp. 42-52, for development of this notion.

21. Flew, *God and Philosophy*, p. 194.

22. *Ibid.*, p. 132.

23. Both theists and atheists have attempted to make hay out of this position. For a short historical survey of the ancient Christian Church Fathers' positions on speaking of the ineffable, see J. R. Illingworth, *The Doctrine of the Trinity* (London: Macmillan, 1907), pp. 102-10; reprinted in I. T. Ramsey, ed., *Words About God: The Philosophy of Religion* (London: SCM Press and New York: Harper and Row, 1971), pp. 15-19. Kai Nielsen has attempted to show that talk of God is incoherent in (among

other places) *Contemporary Critiques of Religion* (New York: Herder and Herder, 1971), ch. six. Nielsen's standards for coherence in this essay are so oriented as to affirm the slightest literal contrariness as incoherence. Nielsen merely takes us back to the problem that Hume left us with in the *Dialogues*: How are we to choose which (admittedly less than perfect) talk to use, the theist's or the atheist's?

2
Non-Cognitivists

Although it may not be totally fair to portray the views discussed in the previous chapter as claiming that believers' talk of God was nonsense, useless and without referent, the similarity of their positions rendered them amenable to treatment as a coherent group. The authors treated in this chapter are more various, although they do share one common tenet: they hold that talk of God by religious people is not factually informative and does not refer to a Being (or Being-Itself), yet can still serve some purpose and be called meaningful. This separation of meaning from facticity characterizes all the positions to be considered in this chapter, but it is, perhaps, most obvious in the work of Benedict (Baruch de) Spinoza (1632-1677).

Benedict Spinoza

As a rationalist metaphysician, Spinoza equated God and Nature: These words were only two different names for the whole. As an unorthodox Jew, he had then to find some use for traditional religious language in the face of the claim that it yielded no knowledge of God-or-Nature. In the *Tractatus Theologico-Politicus*, Spinoza pleaded for understanding, toleration and freedom in religious beliefs on the ground that the prophets of Israel (and religious speakers generally) used language that had weight "only in matters of morality."[1] He attempted to demonstrate this by showing that there was nothing in Scripture that ought to conflict with our ordinary knowledge, for each had its own foundation and each was entirely separate from the other.

Prophecy is the expression of revelation. A prophet does not undertake to communicate knowledge superior to ordinary knowledge to the masses. Rather, he interprets the revelation of God in words and figures that can be understood by them. The Lord did not enlighten the prophets' intellects, but rather appealed to their imaginations so that they could perceive that which went beyond the bounds of the intellect. The prophets "perceived nearly everything in parables and allegories, and clothed spiritual truths in bodily forms, for such is the usual method of the imagination."[2] All prophecy is, according to Spinoza, couched in language that expresses the revelation of God in such a manner as to make it intelligible and forceful for the common people.

Since God cannot deceive the good person—and the prophets were both good and also patently wrong or contradictory on some things—that which God has revealed to them, the essence of their prophecy, cannot be natural knowledge, or speculative knowledge, or spiritual knowledge. Since the prophets had made mistakes in these areas and they were good, the revelation of God must have been in some other area. The revelation—and the essence of prophecy—must bear on charity and morality rather than on knowledge of any sort.

Divine law is natural law. The reward of the divine law is the law itself: To know God and to love him of our own free choice is its own reward. Yet the description of God as a lawgiver is metaphorical, a concession to the understanding of the masses. Spinoza claims that "in reality, God directs all things simply by necessity of his nature and perfection and that his decrees and volitions are eternal truths."[3] Talk of God, as used by religious leaders and religious believers, is finally a popularization of the truth—not itself the truth.

Since divine law is natural law, miracles provide no proof of the existence of God. Miracles are only natural events that the mind cannot readily comprehend. When an event is viewed as miraculous, that simply means that the beholder could not understand what was going on and the event was attributed to the will and power of God for the edification of the masses. It is not through miracles—events that we do not understand—that we come to know God, but only through "phenomena that we clearly and distinctly understand, which heightens our knowledge of God and most clearly indicates his will and decrees."[4] Miracle stories are either tales told for edification of the common folk, or merely odd Hebraic ways of putting things, which today we think of as miracles. The point of these stories is not to give us knowledge of events that are breaking natural laws—why should God break the decrees of his own nature?—but rather to show the greatness of God.

Spinoza lays out similarities and differences in interpreting Scripture and interpreting nature. Just as knowledge of nature is from within nature, so must knowledge of the Bible come from within the Bible. As we import no knowledge from outside nature to understand nature, so we must import nothing from outside Scripture to understand Scripture. The real point of biblical teaching is to promote good living and virtue: "The Divine origin of Scripture must consist solely in its teaching true virtue."[5] In the realm of morals and virtue, the Bible teaches nothing contradictory, according to Spinoza. While some texts may seem contradictory, an interpreter aware of the oddities of Hebrew and cognizant of the context of an assertion will be able to eliminate these. The point of the Bible, especially the utterances of the prophets, is not to communicate facts about the world, but to teach true piety; what is communicated is the *greatness* of God, not who, what, how or where God is.

Scripture is sacred "as long as it is religiously used; if the users cease to be pious, the thing ceases to be sacred. . . . Nothing is in itself absolutely sacred, or profane, or unclean, apart from the mind, but only relative thereto."[6] The Bible does not teach truth for all time because it is a set of works collected and kept alive beyond the time in which they were composed. The meaning of Scripture is not truth, and understanding Scripture does not give us understanding of God or truth. The true meaning of Scripture and of religion is the promotion of righteousness. Spinoza writes:

> If a man, by believing what is true, becomes rebellious, his creed is impious. If by believing what is false, he becomes obedient, his creed is pious; for the true knowledge of God comes not by commandment but by Divine gift. God has

required nothing from man but a knowledge of His Divine
justice and charity, and that not as necessary to scientific
accuracy, but to obedience.[7]

The speculative doctrines of philosophy and the knowledge gained
by science do not matter for religion. What matters is obedience to
God. Only what is necessary to insure that obedience is necessary
for religious talk: that God is supreme, one, omnipresent ruler of
all; that his worship is justice and charity; that those who obey him
are saved; and that he forgives those who repent. All the rest is
unimportant—except when it affects obedience and piety.

Religious language functions to promote piety. For Spinoza,
that was its only meaning. Whether one's religious beliefs were
true or false did not matter. What mattered was how one's talk of
God promoted righteousness. Knowledge of God comes from the
study of nature and of philosophy, but these have nothing to do
with the practical, religious promotion of true virtue. But as we
shall see, the total separation of truth-questions from virtue-
promotion is a problem.[8]

Ludwig Feuerbach

A rather different picture of the meaning of talk about God is
painted by Ludwig Feuerbach (1804-1872) in *The Essence of Christianity*, which he called a "close translation, or, to speak literally,
an empirical or historico-philosophical analysis of Christianity."[9]
While Spinoza had claimed that talk of God is, in the religious
realm, only for insuring morals and not for describing God, Feuerbach argued that talk of God *does* describe—but not some being
called God; rather it speaks of the nature of *man*! Feuerbach saw
man as a being with reason, will and affection. When a man
contemplates an object, he is really becoming acquainted with
himself: "Consciousness of the objective is the self-consciousness
of man."[10] what is called the absolute or God is not some Being,
but the nature of man. When a man thinks or feels the infinite, he
is thinking and feeling his own nature.

Feeling is thy own inward power, but at the same time a power distinct from thee, and independent of thee; it is in thee, above thee; it is itself that which constitutes the objective in thee—thy own being which impresses thee as another being; in short, thy God. How wilt thou, then, distinguish from this objective being within thee another objective being? How wilt thou get beyond thy feeling?[11]

It is the human qualities that are divine, not some being "in the clouds" upon which we project those qualities.

Feuerbach goes on to analyze each of the traditional Christian attributes ascribed to God as projections by man of his own nature on a supersensible being for which there is no evidence and no reason to believe in. He analyzes all the major doctrines of Christianity in this way, too, but his conception of the doctrine of the incarnation shows his approach most explicitly. Feuerbach summarized it as follows:

Hence, only in Christ is the last wish of religion realised, the mystery of religious feeling solved:—solved, however, in the language of imagery proper to religion, for what God is in essence, that Christ is in actual appearance. So far the Christian religion may justly be called the absolute religion. That God, who in himself is nothing else than the nature of man, should also have real existence as such, should be as man an object to the consciousness—this is the goal of religion; and this the Christian religion has attained in the incarnation of God, which by no means is a transitory act, for Christ remains man even after his ascension,—man in heart and man in form, only that his body is no longer an earthly one, liable to suffering.[12]

Feuerbach understands the incarnation as a symbol that expresses the divinity of humanity, not merely the divinity of Christ.

Many questions remain concerning the adequacy of Feuerbach's critique. Setting aside the criticism that he has fallen into the genetic fallacy—which is like understanding a word only in terms of its etymology and beginnings and not in terms of its current use—is his simple, optimistic approach the best available option? Does his analysis entail atheism? With Feuerbach, as with most of the non-cognitivist analysts, the answers to these questions remain obscure, as we shall see later in this chapter.

A more recent approach to the problem of talk of God informed by the positions discussed previously has arisen in the current century. The non-cognitive mode of analysis, a *prescriptive* analysis, attributes some sense to religious talk of God similar to the sense ascribed it by Spinoza and Matthew Arnold (who will appear in the next chapter), but denies a referent to the language, i.e., claims that this talk is not talk of some being or Being. Three influential versions of this approach have appeared.

Richard Bevan Braithwaite

An Empiricist's View of the Nature of Religious Belief by Braithwaite, a philosopher of science, argues that the primary element in religious talk of God is *moral* or *ethical assertion*. Talk of God displays one's intention to live in a certain way:

> Unless a Christian's assertion that God is love (agape)— which I take to epitomize the assertions of the Christian religion—be taken to declare his intention to follow an agapeistic way of life, he could be asked what is the connection between the assertion and the intention, between Christian belief and Christian practice. And this question can always be asked if religious assertions are separated from conduct. Unless religious principles are moral principles, it makes no sense to speak of putting them into practice.[13]

By claiming that religious assertions are declarations of moral policy, Braithwaite copes with a major problem, the distinction of one religion from another. He suggests that the distinguishing characteristics of each will be the set of stories used to induce the following of the recommended policy, suggesting that the following conditions are necessary and sufficient to be a Christian:

A man is not, I think, a professing Christian unless he both proposes to live according to Christian moral principles and associates his intention with thinking of Christian stories; but he need not believe that the empirical propositions presented by the stories correspond to empirical fact.[14]

Braithwaite cites Matthew Arnold as his guide. He avers that Arnold's purpose was " 'cementing the alliance between the imagination and conduct' by regarding the propositional element in Christianity as 'literature' rather than 'dogma.' "[15] Braithwaite suggests that Arnold was at fault for believing that there was a power, called by Arnold the *Eternal not ourselves that makes for righteousness*, to which these literary pieces referred. What is clear is that Braithwaite did not adopt Arnold, but adapted him; while Arnold thought that a reference was necessary for religious talk of God to keep its sense, Braithwaite argues that it is not so. Yet whether eliminating reference is an *improvement* remains to be seen.

Richard M. Hare

The second prescriptivist to be considered is the Oxford moral philosopher Richard M. Hare. Hare suggests that religious talk of God displays the attitudes and intentions of the speaker. Religious language can be understood when one understands what he labels *bliks*. Although he neglects to define this term, his stories show that it means "a fundamental attitude, stance, or presupposition that a person takes to the facts and/or the world." Everyone has a *blik*, and there are many different ones. Some are sane, some insane; some productive, some non-productive. While most of the attitudes one has are amenable to correction, one's *blik* is exceptionally resistant to change; it is fundamental. Hare illustrates his *blik*:

A certain lunatic is convinced that all dons want to murder him. His friends introduce him to all the mildest and most respectable dons that they can find, and after each of them has retired, they say, "You see, he doesn't really want to murder you; he spoke to you in a most cordial manner; surely you are convinced now?" But the lunatic replies, "Yes, but that was only his diabolical cunning; he's really plotting against me the whole time, like the rest of them; I know it I tell you." However many kindly dons are produced, the reaction is still the same.[16]

Hare's point is that "religion" is composed of elements that are evaluative-prescriptive-conative and elements that are factual— and that how we understand the facts is dependent on our *blik*. No series of factual observations is sufficient to falsify a *blik*, but a *blik*, being fundamental, is still important.

Paul M. van Buren

Perhaps the most widely read of the trinity of non-cognitivist empiricist students of religion is the American Paul van Buren. In his *The Secular Meaning of the Gospel*, he relies heavily on the works of Braithwaite and Hare to discuss religious language. His contribution to the "death of God" theology has often been chronicled, but the coherence of *Secular Meaning* with earlier and later works has been ignored.

Van Buren had completed his doctorate under neo-orthodox Protestant theologian Karl Barth. In the preface to the published version of his dissertation he wrote, "This study in Calvin has strengthened my conviction that as Christ is the centre of our faith, so Christology is the determining centre of all theology."[17] This conviction clearly undergirds his subsequent publications as well.

The Secular Meaning of the Gospel begins by surveying Christology up to the council of Chalcedon (451 A.D.). But the understanding the early Christians had of Christ's person and work is not the only one possible, and today is "dated." Van Buren thus turns to a more recent Christology, advocated by some devotees of biblical theology. Their claim is that Jesus is to be understood as *responding* to a *call* to be the "man for others" and he responded completely to that call. The rest of us ought to respond to that call, too, but we cannot do so as well as he did. "But although such an interpretation may be called 'orthodox,' it is still, from the point of view of the theological 'left,' sadly mythological in form, if not in content."[18] Van Buren then takes aim at the theological left—represented by German Scripture scholar Rudolf Bultmann and American theologian Schubert Ogden—objecting that they have "made room for faith without Christ, or at least without a 'Christ' bound up with the historical man Jesus of Nazareth—an interesting, but not original conclusion."[19]

A discussion of various analysts of religious language is undertaken that concludes that the choice of a "non-cognitive, 'blik' conception of faith, rather than of a cognitive conception will be fundamental to our study."[20] He expresses his commitment to a gospel that begins with whatever happened at Easter, and that the straightforward use of the word "God" must be abandoned. Van Buren's view of the analytical position can be formulated in two theses: (1) The language of faith has meaning when it is taken to refer to the Christian way of life; it is not a set of cosmological assertions; (2) a blik, the *discernment* and *commitment* of faith, is by definition something that is lived.[21]

In his examination of the Gospel tradition, van Buren asserts that Jesus was a man of faith and that faith is freedom. Freedom "is not a consequence of faith. It is its logical meaning."[22] What van Buren means by this is that whenever we read the term "faith" we could as well read the term "freedom" for they have the same meaning—one in the religious realm and the other in the secular realm. He goes on to use this equation to analyze the Easter event. According to van Buren, the Gospel for Easter Sunday should be reconstructed to read something like this:

> [The disciples] experienced a discernment situation in which Jesus the free man whom they had known, themselves, and indeed the whole world, were seen in a quite new way. From that moment, the disciples began to possess something of the freedom of Jesus. His freedom began to be "contagious". . . . Because of the new way in which the disciples saw him and because of what had happened to them, the story had to

include the event of Easter. In telling the story of Jesus of
Nazareth, therefore, they told it as a story of the free man
who had set them free.[23]

In the language available to them, the disciples proclaimed the
message. In order to translate that language into the conceptual
framework of modern times, van Buren suggests two guiding principles:

1. Statements of faith are to be interpreted, by means of the
modified verification principle, as statements which express,
describe or commend a particular way of seeing the world,
other men, and oneself, and the way of life appropriate to
such a perspective.

2. The norm of the Christian perspective is the series of
events to which the New Testament documents testify, cen-
tering in the life, death and resurrection of Jesus of
Nazareth.[24]

For instance, the confession "I believe in God, the Father Al-
mighty, Creator of heaven and earth . . ." is to be interpreted not as
a belief about some cosmic event in which God shaped the world,
but rather as the expression of the Christian affirmative attitude
toward the world. Prayer is preparation for action, not petition or
thanksgiving directed to some suprasensible Being. While van
Buren offers a more fleshed-out version of the Christian faith than
either Braithwaite or Hare, his fundamental reliance on their positions renders him amenable to the same sorts of criticisms.

Nine years after the publication of *The Secular Meaning of the
Gospel*, van Buren published *The Edges of Language*. In his later
work the verification principle, whose troubles we noted in the last
chapter, does not reign supreme, exercising linguistic vetoes over
religious meaning. Van Buren's new model for understanding
theological language is a flat-earth image, where theological language lies at the edges of language, along with other strange sorts
of discourse such as puns, humor, metaphysics and paradox. All of
these are in danger, at times, of falling off the edge of language into

the void of nonsense. All of these differ from the "great central plains" of language upon which we all can and do stand: The central plains appear solid and safe, while the "edges" are dangerous.

In using the word "God," what is a speaker doing? Where is he walking? Are there any rules to guide him or signs to tell him where he is going? Van Buren intends to map those rules, as best he can, out in the (so far mostly unmapped) theological back country. The problem is that talk of God seems to demand total commitment on little, if any, evidence, and that modern people have come to believe that in the "plurality of our experience, convictions ought to be held only with the degree of firmness which the evidence and warrants allow."[25] After a reexamination of the prescriptive theories of talk of God, the moral interpretation and the "quasi-metaphysical" interpretation, van Buren rejects them all as inadequate and turns to what he calls a functional analysis. Examining how religious talk functions reveals that we use religious language to express the way we live in the world. It is important that Christianity is a religious way of living that gives a central place to language, for "decisions about language are decisions about life, and changing our ways of speaking changes our way of life."[26]

Van Buren's own model for language is not the "flat-earth" view, but the image he offers is the "platform." The boards of the platform are compared to the rules for using language. We can only add to the platform while we are standing upon it (for it is unclear that the platform of language rests upon any foundation—certainly not a firm one). What we sometimes do is to stretch the meaning of a word so as to use it away from that part of the platform in which it grew up and is at home (for the sports-minded, we could say that this "loses the home-field advantage" for a word—and most words, like most teams, work better at home than somewhere else). Van Buren concludes his examination of some words (mostly nouns) by saying:

> The rules for our use of words permit us in most cases to stretch the application of these words into realms in which they may be less clear than on their home ground, until we come to areas in which they become either utterly ambiguous

or totally unclear. At some point an attempted application of the word loses touch with its rules.[27]

Van Buren is not concerned with meaningless talk—nonsense—but only with that talk which does not fall off the edges of language (somehow suspended above the abyss of nonsense).

But why ought one (or even how can one) abandon the vast central plains to tiptoe gingerly around the edges of language? "A desire, a longing to push out the limits of some particular area of our language, implies that there is a realm of discourse and life in which our ordinary or rule-governed behavior does not seem to be adequate."[28] Whether we see those longings and the accompanying behavior as wise or foolish will depend on our own perspective. No one is required to abandon the central plains, but those who choose not to do so have only the central perspective from which to judge the whole—a perspective that the explorers may (not surprisingly) find rather prosaic.

Van Buren identifies "God-talk" as marking the limits of language. He reviews some of the manifold ways in which religious persons have spoken of God, suggesting that it is problematical to speak of God as if he were another person or object for this option has been vetoed by most Christian theologians. That is, if the placement of the word "God" is as plain as that of "house," "tree" or "chair", then almost all the uses of the word "God" are flawed; talk of God is nothing if it is plain, flat and everyday. But if the place of the word "God" is beyond the limits of language, then the word is meaningless and talk of God is nonsense. So the right place for "God," to be meaningful and profound, must be right on the *edge* of language! Van Buren comments on its meaning:

> If saying "God" is an acknowledgement that one has come to the end of language, if it is a religious way of indicating that one longs to say all that could possibly be said on some matter of great concern, then that is a role which lies just barely but legitimately within our language.[29]

Those who walk only on the broad central plains live in a clear world, but one that the religious person would claim remains safe, secure, dull and shallow. The word "God" functions, then, as an indicator word; it shows that we are in danger of falling into nonsense and it tells those who hear us that what we say is of great importance and meaning to us.

Criticism of the Non-Cognitivists

In van Buren's view of the logic of Christian theistic language, "God" has no reference, though it has a number of uses or meanings. "God" shows that a speaker is *approaching* nonsense, but itself is not nonsense, nor does it *refer to* nonsense. The word "God" indicates to a hearer that what the speaker is saying is clearly of major importance to him or her, but it does not refer to any god. The word "God" indicates the location of the language being used—on the edge—but it does not refer to the edge or to a god who might there appear. Apparently the only differences between A to D below offered in a situation by different speakers (other conditions being the same) is that they display different attitudes:

A: God raised Jesus from the dead.

B: Jesus rose from the dead.

C: The apostles caught Jesus' freedom.

D: The apostles were deluded about what happened on Easter.

We shall also consider the following:

E: Nothing special happened at Easter.

E involves a claim that is opposed to claims involved by A, B, C and D. Is this difference simply one of attitudes, simply a question of the way in which each speaker looks at the world? While the utterer of A or B (certainly), the utterer of C (probably) and the utterer of D (possibly) would take issue with the utterer of E, it would be on the grounds that E had no idea of what happened: The problem is not only attitudinal, but also factual. The utterer of E simply does not know the facts, for something happened that changed the course of Western history. While the differences of A, B, C and D may be attitudinal at root, they are not necessarily so. D and E may have similar attitudes toward what Christians call the

Easter event, but their differences are factual. B and C may agree on some of the facts, but not on all of them; they may also differ in their attitudes toward the facts. A and D have attitudinal difference, but they also have major factual disagreements. Many a stubborn Christian theist still wants to argue with the atheist or the agnostic—not on attitudinal grounds alone, but on the grounds that the atheist or agnostic cannot do justice to all the facts that are witnessed to in utterances like A to D above and in other sorts of religious talk of God.

Generally, this is the sort of problem that the non-cognitivist theories of religious language run up against: They cannot account for the differences between the atheist and the theist in matters of fact—and both would often claim that this sort of difference over what was true and what was false is just what the crucial difference between them was. Talk of God does display attitudes; it is "odd" from the point of view of everyday, flat talk, and should involve some moral claims. But in most cases it claims to do more than that. Non-cognitivist analysis cannot account for differences about the truth of talk of God—and these differences do occur.

Besides sharing the general problem of inability to talk of the truth or falsity of talk of God, each of the modern trio we have discussed here has his own individual problems. Braithwaite's problem is that if the stories that are used to reinforce the intentions of religious people are not believed to be related to actual events, are not understood as telling the truth, but are understood as pious fables, tall tales or legends, how can these stories be held as normative? If they are not factually significant, why believe them? If they have the factual veracity of tales of Santa Claus, why use them to guide your life? While *some* religious language refers to no entity other than the speaker, that does not mean that *all* talk of God takes this form. As Feuerbach has pointed out, some talk of God is autobiographical or projection of man's dreams upon the clouds—but the question still remains, is all of it that? Braithwaite cannot account for those who firmly believe that God is the Creator of heaven and earth in a real way except to claim that those speakers don't know what they are saying.

But if religious stories convey intentions or reinforce them, and religious assertions (e.g., "God is love") express an individual's intentions, what is the meaning of "God is omnipresent," "God is eternal," "God is unchanging"? While the sample that Braithwaite used lends itself to his treatment quite well, many others that are important to traditional Christians cannot be interpreted so easily. What is the intention of the speaker who claims "God is eternal" and tells stories that speak of God's everlastingness? To live a long life? To emulate God's faithfulness? To live as if every moment counts and every moment is of equal worth? Braithwaite's conative analysis falls down because there is no clear connection between most of these utterances and the intention that the speaker is supposedly expressing in uttering them. There are no clear or persuasive guidelines for the "educated hearer" to interpret just what intention a speaker is expressing. While most (if not all) talk of God has a conative aspect, if that is its only sense, can we take it seriously?

Hare's problem is that *bliks*, whatever else they may be, are certainly self-involving, but on what level? "This is the way I view the world; you may view it otherwise, but that is just the difference between you and me." Some cosmological assertions are passionately held to be true, and Hare is finally unable to give an account of how we can differ about these in any reasonable way. Perhaps these assertions are wrong, as Antony Flew holds. But they are made, debated and thought to be true. There is surely something right in understanding talk of God as not straightforwardly empirical, as Hare points out, but his resolution—that faith can be held (as true? or how?) in spite of the facts—goes too far in the direction of denying any reference to the facts in talk of God.

Bliks are also clearly presuppositional. Are all sorts of talk of God presuppositional? I think not. A claim such as "God raised Jesus from the dead" has further presuppositions that go before it: God exists, Jesus exists, Jesus died, etc. Talk of God is not always presuppositional in the way *bliks* —whatever they might be—are.

In a discussion of the post-Resurrection faith (with St. Paul as his example) Hare asks the following question: "What, then, when we are dealing with 'supernatural' facts, is the difference between facts and illusions?"[30] Hare can offer no answer to this question for he is finally unable to account for the differences between faith, delusion and illusion. And these differences count for Christians—and for their strenuous opponents like Flew. From the Christian side, take St. Paul:

> Now if Christ raised from the dead is what has been preached, how can some of you be saying that there is no resurrection of the dead? If there is no resurrection of the dead, Christ himself cannot have been raised, and if Christ has not been raised then our preaching is useless and your believing is useless; indeed, we are shown up as witnesses who have committed perjury before God, because we swore in evidence before God that he had raised Christ to life. For if the dead are not raised, Christ has not been raised, and if Christ has not been raised, you are still in your sins. And what is more serious, all who have died in Christ have perished. If our hope in Christ has been for this life only, we are the most unfortunate of all people. (1 Cor. 15:12-19)

This argument holds whether it is presented in the Hellenic world of the first century or the modern world of the twentieth. It makes a difference whether we believe in truth or illusion. That it is difficult to differentiate between the two in cases like this does not mean that it cannot or should not be attempted. "If Christ has not been raised, our faith is useless and we are still in our sins." To the Christian it makes a difference whether Resurrection is fact or illusion—and Hare fails to give a theory that can account for this difference.

Paul van Buren, who bases much of his work—almost all of *The Secular Meaning of the Gospel*—on Hare and Braithwaite, is vulnerable to the criticisms discussed above. In terms of the discussion among analytical philosophers of religion, it is also clear that he has misunderstood the work of Ian T. Ramsey (whom we shall discuss in chapter four), taking his work as a "noncognitivist" interpretation of religious language whereas Ramsey clearly intended to understand the logic of religious language as involving claims to truth. *The Edges of Language* clarifies and enlarges the analysis of *The Secular Meaning of the Gospel* but does not move beyond the position set up in the earlier book in any significant way. His work cannot do justice to talk of God because

he merely brushes aside those questions that are the thorniest
—the questions of reference to an entity or Power not ourselves
that acts in or influences our history, and the questions of the
differences between truth, illusion and delusion in matters most
important to the believers. Like Hare and Braithwaite, van Buren
gives an adequate account of some of the uses of talk of God, but
not all of them; and he cannot give an adequate account of the
believers' claims that their talk of God is *true*.

Three further problems occur in van Buren's work. He claims
that beliefs ought to be held with the degree of firmness that the
evidence and warrants allow. But, as with the verification principle, what evidence is there for believing *that* claim? Is there sufficient compelling evidence to allow that claim to be supported? Or
do we have the same problem that we saw with Antony Flew in
chapter one—that the claim itself precludes evidence for itself. In
the end, such sweeping guides tend to be self-defeating if understood as the basic foundation for our talking.

"Decisions about language are decisions about life, and changing our ways of speaking changes our way of life," says van Buren.[31] Again, we have a sweeping claim: Is *every* decision to use
one phrase rather than another a decision about the way one is
going to live? In a trivial sense, certainly, for we could speak other
than the way we do about almost everything we see and do. But if
this claim is not trivial, it needs to be clarified so we can see *which*
decisions about language are important decisions about our way of
life. Also, is the choice of words the result of decision? May it be
the result of habit and training? *Some* of our talk is *not* rooted in a
conscious decision, and *some* of our possibilities are *not* chosen by
us, but given to us. Van Buren needs to be much more clear on just
what his claims mean and how he intends them to be understood.
Until this is clarified, the precise scope of his theory cannot be
determined.

Finally, the platform view of language (or the flat-earth view,
as I have characterized it) leads to various sorts of trouble. Perhaps
the most crucial one is an inability to account for all the ordinary
meanings of the word "world." Van Buren writes, "The wider the
spectrum of language a man employs . . . the richer is the world in
which he finds himself."[32] In one sense of the word "world" this is

quite true, for we speak of our thought-world and talk about the extent of that which influences us and of that which we influence as our "world." However, there is a world beyond my world, a world to which I want to refer and to relate in my language. If *my* world cannot talk of God and *the* world is divine (or that in which we live, move and have our being is God), then so much the worse for *my* world, for it cannot tell the whole truth about *the* world. If *my* world talks of God and *the* world is not a divine cosmos but a random chaos, then *my* world is an illusion in light of *the* world and can neither show nor say the truth. While van Buren is correct in saying that the broader the language a man can use is, the richer his world is, he says nothing about the truth or the falsity of either the rich world of the person who walks at the edges of language or of the narrower world of the person who remains in the central plains. The problem is that van Buren can account for neither shallow truths nor rich falsehoods. This suggests that van Buren's whole model of language is a problem, and his inadequate understanding of religious language is an outgrowth of an inadequate theory of language in general.

Finally, we return to Feuerbach, for whom talk of God is really talk of mankind, a position that seems curiously similar to the ones just considered, but crucially different in that Feuerbach speaks not of "a man" but of the "nature of man" in his formulation. What of the adequacy of his position? Neo-orthodox theologian Karl Barth, in an essay incorporated into the Harper Torchbook edition of the English translation of *The Essence of Christianity,* writes, "Anyone who knew that we men are evil from head to foot and anyone who reflected that we must die, would recognize it to be the most illusory of all illusions to suppose that the essence of God is the essence of man."[33] This can be understood in two ways. Either Feuerbach is right in considering the essence of God as the essence of man but didn't go far enough, for he should have also included the devil as a projection of the essence of man (of course, Barth did not intend this, but a Feuerbachian might revise Feuerbach's position this way), or Feuerbach's theories can speak of some of (or perhaps all of) our concepts of God, but cannot speak of God himself. Feuerbach may criticize *my* world, but is that a criticism of *the* world? In other words, Feuerbach's maintaining that "God as God, that is, a being not finite, not human, not materially conditioned, not phenomenal, is only an object of thought"[34] may only imply that whatever we say about God cannot be adequate to describe him. But is the impossibility of description due to the fact that God is too great to be described or that there is nothing to be described? The answer to this question makes a difference, and Feuerbach, like the later non-cognitivist interpreters of religious talk of God, cannot account for this difference.

While it is clear that Spinoza's position is not even adequate to account for the various forms of language in the Bible, two sorts of things can be learned from his work. First, religious and philosophical uses of the word "God" may differ in intents and purposes; talk of God in philosophy may do different sorts of things than talk of God does in religion. Secondly, Spinoza made clear that there are similarities between moral and religious talk; however, most would find fault with him for identifying them.

All the theorists of religious language considered in this chapter have suggested various senses for talk of God and affirmed that this talk has no reference, in spite of the fact that it seems to refer to God and the fact that most theists heartily believe that this reference, if true, makes a difference in the world. If language, to refer to something, must *describe* it adequately, then many of the criticisms of these theorists are on the right track. But if language does other work besides describing, if it can refer even though it does not describe, if there is a place for analogy and symbol and for pointing at that of which we cannot speak adequately in descriptive terms, then there is the possibility that the problem of the reference of talk of God cannot be dismissed so lightly. And in fact that is the case.

Consider an internal combustion engine. I can refer to it without describing it adequately, i.e., laying out the schematics for its construction, describing the valves, cylinders, pistons, rings and their functions, etc. I can make mistakes in my representation of it (e.g., construing a four-stroke engine as a two-stroke engine), and that representation is flawed (at best). I can make mistakes in reference (taking an automatic transmission to be an engine), and then I am wrong (at worst). Yet even in some circumstances, e.g., answering "What makes the car go?" I am not *totally* wrong, though both reference and representation are not adequate.

Can we say the same sort of thing about religious talk of God? Yes. Perhaps believers are wrong in thinking that there is a God for their talk to refer to, but they are not wrong about that talk's referring; the question is whether it does so successfully. In the next two chapters we will discuss theorists who take the problem of reference seriously and try to discover in what ways talk about God can possibly refer to an entity or Being who acts in or influences our history. Theologians and philosophers treated later do not necessarily ignore the sorts of considerations made by theorists discussed in this chapter, but attempt, for the most part, to move beyond the non-cognitive analyses to positions that can account for both the manifold senses of talk of God and the importance of the problem of reference.

Notes

1. Benedict de Spinoza, *Tractatus Theologico-Politicus*, in *The Chief Works of Benedict de Spinoza*, trans. R. H. M. Elwes (London: George Bell and Sons, 1889), I, p. 8.

2. *Ibid.*, p. 25.

3. *Ibid.*, p. 65.

4. *Ibid.*, p. 86.

5. *Ibid.*, p. 100.

6. *Ibid.*, p. 167.

7. *Ibid.*, p. 198.

8. Matthew Arnold, who will be discussed in the next chapter (for reasons that will become clear there), was influenced by Spinoza and clearly appreciated his work in "Spinoza and the Bible" in *Essays in Criticism* (New York: Macmillan, 1905). Arnold ignores (as I have) Spinoza's conclusions on the relationship of the churches to the state. Arnold plays down Spinoza's metaphysical doctrines and emphasizes the imaginary voice of God as the true voice of God. The truth of this cannot be demonstrated, but can be affirmed to be true on the basis of practice if it produces piety and obedience, according to Arnold.

9. Ludwig Feuerbach, *The Essence of Christianity*, trans. George Eliot (New York: Harper and Row, 1957), p. xxxiii.

10. *Ibid.*, p. 5.

11. *Ibid.*, p. 11. This point is directed most acutely at F. D. E.

Schleiermacher. If theology's doctrines are completely derivable from man's religious consciousness of feeling absolutely dependent, then it seems obvious that these doctrines need be no more than doctrines concerning man's consciousness. Schleiermacher bases his theology on that feeling; Feuerbach drew the conclusion that that upon which man feels absolutely dependent need be no other than himself.

12. *Ibid.*, p. 145.

13. Richard Bevan Braithwaite, *An Empiricist's View of the Nature of Religious Belief* (London: Cambridge University Press, 1955); reprinted entirely in *Christian Ethics and Contemporary Philosophy*, ed. I. T. Ramsey (London: SCM Press, 1966), p. 63.

14. *Ibid.*, p. 68. The differences between the religions are the different stories used to evoke or reinforce a way of life. The Buddhist story set, for instance, will include stories surrounding the enlightenment of Gautama. See chapter one for a discussion of Flew's criticism of this sort of position.

15. *Ibid.*, p. 69. The quotation is from the preface to *God and the Bible*.

16. R. M. Hare, "Theology and Falsification," in *New Essays in Philosophical Theology*, ed. A. Flew and A. MacIntyre (London: SCM Press, 1955; New York: Macmillan, 1970), pp. 99-100. Also see Hare's "Religion and Morals" in *Faith and Logic*, ed. B. Mitchell (London: Allen and Unwin, 1957).

17. Paul van Buren, *Christ in Our Place: The Substitutionary Character of Calvin's Doctrine of Reconciliation* (Grand Rapids: Wm. B. Eerdmans, 1956), p. vii.

18. Paul van Buren, *The Secular Meaning of the Gospel: Based on an Analysis of Its Language* (New York: Macmillan, 1963, paperback edition, 1966), p. 55.

19. *Ibid.*, p. 63.

20. *Ibid.*, p. 97.

21. *Ibid.*, pp. 99-100. It also should be noted that what van Buren identifies as the verification principle, i.e., "the meaning of a word is its use in its context" (104), is not the verification principle. His study is informed, however, by his acceptance of a version of the soft form of the verification principle, i.e., a sentence is meaningful if it can be falsified. For discussion of the problems that this principle encountered see R. W. Ashby, "Verifiability Principle," in *The Encyclopedia of Philosophy*, ed. P. Edwards (New York: Macmillan and Free Press, 1967), VIII, pp. 240-246, and the literature Ashby cites.

22. Van Buren, *The Secular Meaning of the Gospel*, p. 124.

23. *Ibid.*, p. 134.

24. *Ibid.*, p. 156.

25. Paul van Buren, *The Edges of Language: An Essay in the Logic of a Religion* (New York: Macmillan, 1972). He cites Van A. Harvey, *The Historian and the Believer* (New York: Macmillan, 1966) as his source for

this point. This is correct if convictions have the same status as hypotheses, but it is not true if they do not. See the discussions of this in my criticism of van Buren and the discussions of D. Z. Phillips and J. W. McClendon and J. M. Smith in chapters three and five.

26. Van Buren, *The Edges of Language*, p. 69.

27. *Ibid.*, p. 95.

28. *Ibid.*, p. 112. While this may be an excellent motive for so moving, is this also a reason? A psychologist may explain my motives differently from the way I would give my reasons for doing a certain action. Van Buren is not clear which this is. And are there other reasons? Or is van Buren inferring the existence of a "realm" from a state of mind? Or are we only describing our state of mind and prescribing actions to be taken? On all these points van Buren is not clear.

29. *Ibid.*, pp. 144-45.

30. Hare, "Religion and Morals," p. 184.

31. Van Buren, *The Edges of Language*, p. 69.

32. *Ibid.*, p. 100.

33. Feuerbach, *The Essence of Christianity*, p. xxvii.

34. *Ibid.*, p. 35.

3
Forebears and Fideists

The theories discussed in the first two chapters shared one claim: that talk of God cannot be reasonably claimed to be true. Although the non-cognitivists discovered that talking of God had other meanings than telling the truth, most religious believers would find that their accounts have missed a crucial point. Believers at least intend to refer to that of which they speak: God. The evaluative question is whether their language carries out their intentions.

This chapter examines a group of theologians characterizable as "cognitivist" in that they find both senses to and a reference for talking of God. The first two theorists, however, are not twentieth-century empiricists. St. Thomas Aquinas (1224?-1274), as the father of much Christian theology, deserves consideration; additionally, he was sensitive, in his own way, to questions of language. Matthew Arnold (1822-1888), British poet, educator and literary critic, also had constructive criticism to offer about the theological uses of the Scriptures. Since he has been claimed as the father of the non-cognitivist approach to religious language, he deserves consideration as much as Aquinas or Hume. But he belongs among those who find a reference for talk of God. After considering these two forebears, we can return to modern empiricists again.

St. Thomas Aquinas

Although he made references to talking of God throughout his works, a crucial point is made in the *Summa Theologica*, in Part I, Question XIII, "The Names of God."[1] There he affirmed that

43

God can be named or referred to insofar as we can understand him through nature by the way of eminence or the way of negation. The way of eminence notes that while we call a person just, we do not call that person "justice"; we know various just people and we can infer what justice is and apply that eminently to God. The way of negation attempts to show that finally God is beyond comparison to all finite things and that by knowing the finite we can know what God is not. Although these ways can lead us to name God, he finally remains beyond our understanding because none of the names captures him.[2]

God is said to have many names—Goodness, Truth, Wisdom—that are not synonymous with the "same" names as applied to finite creatures. In God these perfections pre-exist "unitedly and simply, whereas in creatures, they are received divided and multiplied."[3] Since God is infinitely greater than his creatures, and since the perfections exist in God in a way rather different from the way they exist in man, to say that God is good has a different sense from saying that a man is good or describing some food as good. Thomas claims a special status for talk of God, an analogical status:

> For in analogies the idea is not, as it is in univocals, one and the same; yet it is not totally diverse as in equivocals; but the name which is thus used in a multiple sense signifies various proportions to some one thing: e.g., healthy, applied to urine, signifies the sign of animal health; but applied to medicine, it signifies the cause of the same health.[4]

The goodness we can see in creatures is imperfect. But to talk of the goodness of God is to talk of perfect goodness. So, although attributing goodness to God is not the same as attributing goodness to a person (that would be univocal or synonymous attribution), neither is the goodness of God *totally* unrelated to the goodness of a person (that would be an equivocation). Because God is the ultimate cause of goodness in creation, the *proper* way to talk of his goodness is analogically, denying both that his goodness is totally like human goodness or totally unlike it.

Aquinas claimed that we understand some words on the basis

of an action that we perceive. His example was that we understand the word stone *(lapis)* because it has acted to hurt the foot *(loedit pedem)*. Analogically we perceive the world and understand it as the result of God's creative act. This creation thus can lead us to talk of that which exists "above all things, the principle of all things, and removed from all things."[5] Of course our imperfect wisdom can perceive the divine wisdom only imperfectly and our imperfect minds can only understand the divine mind dimly, but this is appropriate for analogical knowledge—it is the best that analogy can do.

The most proper name for God is HE WHO IS (Exodus 3:14) because, says St. Thomas, it best symbolizes God:

> For it does not signify some form, but being itself *(ipsum esse)*. Hence, since the being of God is His very essence (which can be said of no other being), it is clear that among other names this one most properly names God; for everything is named according to its essence.[6]

This name also is said to be most proper for it connotes the universality of God and the fact that all is present (there is no past or future) to God.

For St. Thomas, then, all our talk of God is at best analogical: We infer his perfections (dimly) from the "incomplete, fractured" perfections we see in creation. We can speak of him analogically only because he has made us. However, "analogy" is a rather slippery term. We have been able to say what it is not, but can we say what it is? David Burrell suggests the following:

> Indeed, for Aquinas it seems to refer to any manner of establishing a notion too pervasive to be defined or too fundamental or exalted to be known through experience. More often than not, this is accomplished via examples designed to point up enough relevant aspects of these notions to use them responsibly. The word coined for this technique was *manuductio*.[7]

But this leading on by examples, this "taking us by the hand" to go beyond our own experience, is a procedure at which some may balk. In other words, it may be considered a step beyond the rational by some, a step many may be unwilling to take. And if we are to go beyond our experience, which aspect of our multifaceted experience are we to take as the key to open the door to the truth about God or the ultimate? Which examples ought we to use? Which human and creaturely attributes are perfections to be ascribed to God? As Hume has shown in his *Dialogues Concerning Natural Religion*, the analogical step is always a precarious one and may, indeed, be one that gives the illusion of truth rather than truth.[8]

But Aquinas was building on centuries of Christian experience. As Burrell put it, "Aquinas worked in the context of belief and breathed the very air of faith. . . ."[9] In that atmosphere, many of the problems raised by David Hume and others (who breathed rather different air) simply did not occur. Aquinas had no real difficulty concerning either the sense or the reference of talk of God. The sense of God-talk is analogical; its reference is to the God of the Judaeo-Christian tradition, JHWH, who is the creative source of all there is. Over seven hundred years after Aquinas' death, we too breathe somewhat different air and cannot assume that he has offered the final solution to the problems of the sense and reference of talk of God. While Thomas is certainly an inspiration, his solution to the problem of talk of God is no longer adequate.

Matthew Arnold

Matthew Arnold was also an inspiration—but to R. B. Braithwaite and R. M. Hare, whose theories of talk of God were treated in the previous chapter. Arnold, like Aquinas, had discovered both a sense and a reference for talk of God. To understand his claim properly we need to understand his primary task: removing the gloss that the churches have added to the teaching of the Bible.

Arnold was opposed to any theory that claimed that the salvation toward which religion aims is "unquestionably annexed to a right knowledge of the Godhead."[10] Arnold understood the Bible to be using the word "God" (in most cases) not as "a term of science or exact knowledge, but a term of poetry and eloquence, a term *thrown out*, so to speak, at a not fully grasped object of the speaker's consciousness, a literary term, in short."[11] Hence, understanding "God" and what it refers to in a literal or scientific way is wrong-headed. Since the Bible is concerned not with right doctrines, but rather with right conduct, the attempts made by dogmatic theologians to demand assent to a right doctrine of God by all those who would be saved is misplaced. Arnold argued:

> And so, when we are asked, what is the object of religion?—let us reply: *Conduct.* And when we are asked further, what is conduct?—let us answer: *Three-fourths of life.*
>
> And certainly we need not go far about to prove that conduct, or "righteousness," which is the object of religion, is in a special manner the object of Bible-religion. The word "righteousness" is the master-word of the Old Testament.[12]

Since the proper objective of religion is the righteousness of its adherents, religion is similar to morality. In fact, Arnold defined religion as "morality touched by emotion."[13] The demands that adherents assent to rational and speculative doctrines, made by church leaders, miss the point. Theological speculation has attempted to make poetry into science, emotion into knowledge, and the revelation of the Eternal into rationality. Arnold claimed that *conduct* was the key—and theological speculation is superfluous since it fails to motivate proper conduct or enhance righteousness.

The Old Testament presented the story of the people of Israel who, instead of following righteousness for its own sake, began to aspire after righteousness as a means to lead to the goal of political triumph. They had begun to take the poetry of life as literal truth. This blunder led to dreams of triumph and away from hungering and thirsting after righteousness. Of the belief in the eventual political triumph of the Jews, Arnold wrote:

> It is a kind of fairy-tale, which a man tells himself, which no one, we grant, can prove impossible to turn out true, but which no one, also can prove to be true. It is . . . belief beyond what is certain and verifiable. . . . *Extra-belief*, that

which we hope, augur, imagine, is the poetry of life, and has
the rights of poetry. But it is not science; and yet it tends
always to imagine itself science, to substitute itself for science, to make itself the ground of the very science out of
which it has grown.[14]

The problem, as Arnold saw it, was that the churches demanded
assent to "extra-belief" *(aberglaube)* as if it were certain, verifiable, literal truth.

Arnold did not claim that it was necessarily *wrong* to hold such
beliefs. On the contrary, some may find them useful: "The object
of religion is conduct; and if a man helps himself in his conduct by
taking an object of hope and presentiment as if it were an object of
certainty, he may even be said to gain thereby an advantage."[15]
The danger is that such a belief will harden into dogmatism or
legalism. And to believe that matters of poetic *aberglaube* are
certainties is to blunder.

The Apostles' record of Jesus is also laced with poetic language. Arnold claimed that the New Testament record was normative and coherent not because it was infallible, but rather because it
was consistent: Each writer was attempting to promote righteousness. Arnold's approach to the message of the New Testament was
summarized in the following:

And the conjunction of the three in Jesus—the method of
inwardness and the secret of self-renunciation, working in
and through this element of mildness—produced a total impression ineffable and indescribable for the disciples, as also
it was irresistible to them, but at which their descriptive
words, words like this *"sweet reasonableness,"* and like *"full
of grace and truth,"* are thrown out and aimed.[16]

The words that they used were like pitches hurled at an unstrikable
target. Even the best words couldn't portray their lord with infallible, irreformable certainty.

As the Apostles died and the immediate remembrance of Jesus
faded away, the record became normative. But what was held as
normative was not only the method and secret of Jesus, but also the
aberglaube of the Apostles that hid and carried that message.

What happened then was that the Christian religion was made "to stand on its apex instead of its base. Righteousness is supported on ecclesiastical dogma, instead of ecclesiastical dogma being supported on righteousness."[17] Arnold claimed that the proper interpretation of the teaching of Jesus (his method and secret) would show that it was aiming not toward right belief, but toward right conduct. He noted that such a claim was not absolutely demonstrable: "It is a maintainable thesis that the theological dogmas of the Trinity, the Incarnation, and the Atonement underlie the whole Bible."[18] The criteria to which Arnold proposed to appeal to decide which claim was better are pragmatic:

> Does experience, as it widens and deepens, make for this or that thesis, or make against it? And the great thing against any such thesis as [the traditional approach to the Bible] is, that the more we know of the history of the human spirit and its deliverances, the more we have reason to think such a thesis improbable, and it loses hold on our assent more and more. On the other hand, the great thing, as we believe, in favour of such a construction as we put upon the Bible is, that experience, as it increases, constantly confirms it; and that, though it cannot *command* assent, it will be found to *win* assent more and more.[19]

Arnold urged Christians to quit quibbling over old doctrines, to ignore revisions intended to breathe new life into old dogmas, and to turn their attention to what is important: righteousness.

Arnold concluded that while conduct may be three-fourths of life, the other fourth—culture and science—was interdependent with conduct. "And, therefore, simple as the Bible and conduct are, still culture seems to be required for them,—required to prevent our mis-handling them and sophisticating them."[20] Thus, since God is the power that makes for righteousness, he also is properly to be called "the Eternal Power, not ourselves, by which all things fulfill the law of their being." God is concerned primarily with conduct, but also with all of life and with all there is. And the acknowledgement of the power of God is the key difference between Arnold and those modern thinkers—especially Braithwaite—who take him as their godfather.

Braithwaite put the difference between himself and Arnold succinctly and well: Arnold "regarded *the Eternal not ourselves that makes for righteousness* more dogmatically than fictionally."[21] Indeed he did! Arnold thought that such a power that makes for righteousness was empirically discoverable and that to consider that power as primary would put the Bible and religion on a solid empirical base. Then the *aberglaube* could indeed be based on that power, but happily recognized as the poetry of life, as *aberglaube*. Arnold acknowledged that the Eternal is usually understood in anthropomorphic terms and he would permit that—if anthropomorphisms are recognized as poetry rather than literal truth. But Arnold—unlike Braithwaite—claimed that there must be at least one true dogma, whose truth was discoverable empirically, to support the encouragement of righteousness and to ground the poetry of life.

The sense Matthew Arnold gave to religious language is clearly moral: the encouragement of right conduct. But he did not do away with the claim that this language also referred; and he discovered, he thought, just what that language talked of (though sometimes poetically): a Power discoverable in the context of human life, a Power that encourages righteousness. Arnold could not, on his theory, say any more literally about that Power. He could only throw words at it in poetry and languages akin to poetry. On Arnold's terms, talk of God must do two things: (1) refer to the Power that makes for righteousness, and (2) encourage right conduct. If it stopped doing either of these, or attempted to do much more, it would fail.

However, the question we must ask is whether religious talk of God is limited in its *sense* to encouraging right conduct. Is that the *only* useful meaning of talk of God? Most religious people and most religious theorists would hesitate to make this claim. Talk of God must have other senses than encouraging or discouraging certain forms of conduct; if it does not, then is it any different at all from ethics? Certainly religious and ethical language share similarities, but that does not mean that they are identical. Matthew Arnold has discovered one meaning for talk of God. We need to discover what other senses or uses talk of God has.

Aquinas and Arnold, each in his own way, has shown us a sense for talk of God. Each has claimed that such talk also refers to a God whose effects can be discerned in and through the world. But each has not justified his claims in a way that remains adequate in the twentieth century. Philosophy and theology have come a long way since the time of Arnold—and even further since the time of Aquinas. What we need to do is to examine some theorists who are aware of that long road and who offer positions adequate to account for talk of God as used by religious believers. One of the more recent attempts to account for religious talk of God was made by Willem F. Zuurdeeg, who was born in Holland, taught in the United States, and offered an account for talk of God in the context of both empiricism and existentialism.

Willem F. Zuurdeeg

Zuurdeeg, in *An Analytical Philosophy of Religion*, examined talk of God in the context of a complex theory of language in general. He distinguished three basic sorts of language: "use-language," "is-language," and "employ-language." When someone is using language as a tool, "a specific language, according to specified, strict rules, for definite purposes,"[22] this is "use-language." A scientist offering a hypothesis to account for some phenomena speaks impersonally and utters "use-language." Zuurdeeg is, for the most part, uninterested in "use-language" and believes that it has little role in understanding religion.

The second type of language Zuurdeeg describes expresses the speaker's *convictions*. "Is-language" is a crucial element in religious language, and to show the importance of "is-language," he defines its content in terms of convictions:

> We take the term "conviction" to mean all persuasions concerning the meaning of life; concerning good and bad; concerning gods and devils; concerning representations of the ideal man, the ideal state, the ideal society; concerning the meaning of history, of nature, and of the All.[23]

A conviction is properly expressed in "is-language" for it says who one *is*—not only intellectually, but as a whole.

We receive our convictions from outside of ourselves; we do

not make them up from "whole cloth." In this process of getting a conviction, an individual ("convictus" is Zuurdeeg's word) is overcome by a convictor whose worthiness is promoted by witnessing authorities. Zuurdeeg believed that individuals with different convictions were convinced by different convictors with different witnesses. One may be convinced of the coming of the classless society (convictor) by the work of Marx and Engels (witnesses). Another may be convinced of the fatherhood of God and the brotherhood of man (convictor) as proclaimed by Jesus and Adolf Harnack (witnesses). These convictional differences are differences in what people ARE. And we ARE different in that we have been convinced by or overcome by different powerful convictors with different witnesses in different situations.

One's convictions are marked by an absence of doubt. Besides the unique way in which one gets a conviction, the certitude with which one holds it differs from the certitude with which one holds a scientific, hypothetical belief. Distinguishing "is-language" from "use-language" by the different sorts of certitude each has (as well as origin), Zuurdeeg wrote:

> The crucial point is that convictional certitude is something different in kind from scientific certitude, something *sui generis*. There is nothing lacking in the certitude of a Moslem that Allah is his God. If this kind of certitude can be fruitfully compared with scientific and mathematical certitude at all, it should be said that convictional certitude is so overwhelming (notice the being-overcome element) that the believer in many instances gives his life for his Cause. The whole person is involved, including his very existence, whereas mathematical and scientific certitude refers solely to the intellect. In short, a discussion of convictional certitude in terms either of probability or qualification of intellectual reasons by sentiment misses the point.[24]

And following from this, Zuurdeeg can claim that the crucial difference between ordinary beliefs or knowledge and convictional belief is that "whereas we *use* a scientific terminology, we *are* our convictions."[25]

Zuurdeeg is not clear on what *being one's convictions* means. However, it is clear that he is attempting to differentiate between that language one uses impersonally and that language that expresses one's ultimate concerns, those beliefs that form and shape one's whole life. While it is hard to see just what Zuurdeeg means, it is clear that the distinction between hypothesis and conviction that he makes is a crucial one for understanding talk of God.

While much of religious language is "is-language" and much of scientific language is "use-language," a third category is needed to account for theological language. Zuurdeeg defines "employ-language" by contrasting it to the other sorts of language he has discussed:

> Employ-language is akin to is-language in that it is related to and tries to express the personality center in regard to matters of ultimate importance. Employ-language is akin to use-language in that it implies an element of distance, of reflection. Employ-language differs from is-language because of this reflective element.[26]

In other words, what we do here is to speak reflectively, employing language to give an account of life.

The problem here is that *all* language can be seen as attempting to give an explanation of life or contributing to an explanation of the meaning of life. How is employ-language finally different from the other sorts of language? Or are all languages finally theological? Can employ-language ever express one's convictions, i.e., can one's convictions ever come about as a result of reflective thinking? Since the latter seems to be the case, at least occasionally, Zuurdeeg cannot account for some of the distinctions that he needs to make to lay out a theory of language that is adequate to account for the various languages that we use.

Zuurdeeg's discussion of a crucial Christian claim serves to show that is-language and use-language are not so separate as he has made them seem:

> If a Christian says: "I believe that nearly twenty centuries ago Jesus Christ lived, and died, and rose again," he does not

intend to make a cognitive statement, but to repeat the old recital, be it in an abbreviated and flat form. This is not to deny that the sentence has some cognitive implications, but these are not the focus of the believer's interest. What is required in the Hebrew and Christian faiths is therefore not a belief in the truth of cognitive sentences, but a willingness to repeat the old recital. Such sentences are not primarily cognitive, but convictional. The belief in them is *not a condition* of faith, but *an integral part of it.*[27]

But is this correct? Would most Christians and Jews recognize themselves as totally ignoring the cognitive implications in reciting their creeds? And while belief in some facts may not be a condition of faith, is it not possible that some beliefs about some facts may be *destructive* of faith? Zuurdeeg's analysis here is simply inadequate to show how faith and facts are sometimes interrelated.

Part of Zuurdeeg's claim is credible: Facts are not a sufficient ground for religious faith, and one is rarely argued into or out of faith. Usually we are grabbed or converted. Yet some cognitive beliefs do indeed preclude some convictions, e.g., the discovery of a body proved to be Jesus' would certainly shake the faith of most Christians. Not all convictions are amenable to having their foundations shaken in this way, but some are; and Zuurdeeg is unable to show how such shaking is possible. The absolute dichotomy between is-language and use-language, between convictional and hypothetical claims, involves the claim that these different types of language cannot conflict with each other. But since they do conflict in practice, the theory is rendered very dubious.

Interestingly, Zuurdeeg tacitly admits the problems with and some of the inadequacies of his position, especially concerning the problem of reference. While religious talk of God will clearly be, on Zuurdeeg's terms, the expression of a conviction, a belief that makes us what we are, and thus have a clear sense, what of the reference of convictions? Zuurdeeg claims two references, to the trans-empirical reality (the classless state, God, the devil, etc.) and to a matrix of historical events (the Bolshevik revolution, the life of Jesus, the "revelation" to Anton le Vey, etc.). In holding that the convictor exerts power over the believer, Zuurdeeg implies that there is a reference for all convictional language. One part of this reference—to the historical—may even undermine a conviction. But what of the trans-empirical realities that grab people? All we can say is that we know our convictor because that convictor has grabbed us! Exactly how we might give consent to this assault is unclear. There are no grounds for assent, resistance or any exercise of reasonableness. Whatever reasons we might give for accepting a new conviction are actually "pronouncements of the glory and majesty of the new convictor."[28] Zuurdeeg notes that some religious communities may find his analysis uncomfortable. More than that, I think, many religious communities would be unwilling to give allegiance to a *totally* a-rational foundation for their claims. What we need is an analysis that can account for all of religious talk of God, noting its reasonable—and unreasonable —components and its claims to refer to the God of Abraham, Isaac, Jacob and Jesus.

Zuurdeeg's approach to the problems of religious language was informed by a rather complex theory of language-in-general, that wove strands from analytical philosophy and from continental existentialism into a rope exceedingly strong in some areas and exceedingly weak in others. His insights, especially the implicit recognition that talk of God may have many senses, are important. His notion that talk of God cannot be extracted from the situation in which that talk arose without doing an injustice to it is an important step forward. But the problems of a commitment to existentially reconstructed religious liberalism, an attempt to do everything in one book on religious and other convictional language, and a confused theory of language render Zuurdeeg's work an interesting failure.

Donald D. Evans

Donald Evans, trained at Oxford, offered a theory of religious language in his important book *The Logic of Self-Involvement*, which relied on the work of Oxford philosopher of language John L. Austin for its philosophical background. Austin had noted that some of our words actually *do work*. For instance, when I say "I promise you that I will be there at noon" something new comes into existence merely by the saying of the words: a promise. Given that you have injured me, when I say "I forgive you" you *are* forgiven; when a policeman says "I arrest you" you *are* arrested; when the judge says "I sentence you to thirty days in jail" you *are* sentenced; when the priest says "This is my body" this *is* (or so Catholics believe) Christ's body. At first Austin thought that he had discovered a philosophically virgin realm of language, a realm he called "performative." With this sort of talk, he contrasted our ordinary flat statements as "constative." His whole theory, contained in lectures published after his death, was *How To Do Things With Words*.[29] But he was noting that he was having trouble finding an ordinary flat statement, as discussed in his eleventh lecture, and that his neat dual classification had broken down. For we also *do* something with our statements—we state! Austin then proceeded to develop a much more pluralistic theory in which he divided the speech-act into three constituent parts: the words (the locution), what act the words performed (the illocution, which could be all of the performatives [Austin easily found over two hundred acts we do with our words] he had found earlier) and the effects that the illocutionary act had (the perlocution—which effects could be intended or unintended). Austin then, very tentatively, grouped the sorts of illocutionary acts one could perform into five general categories: verdictives (typically, the giving of a verdict by a jury and its analogous acts in other contexts), exercitives (typically, exercising a power, such as voting, enacting, warning), commissives (typically, promising or other actions in which one makes a commitment), behabatives (a miscellaneous group having to do with attitudes and social behavior, such as congratulating, commending, etc.), and expositives (these acts make plain just how our sayings fit into the course of an argument or conversation, such as replying, conceding, assuming, presuming, etc.). He noted that there were many overlaps, marginal cases and awkward uses that fit in none of the categories exactly.[30]

Evans adopted Austin's methods, revised his categories and developed a theory about self-involving talk. In a later article he summarized the crucial elements of self-involving language in contrast to "neutral" language. Evans wrote:

> A self-involving assertion is one which commits the person who asserts it or accepts it to further action, or which implies that he has an attitude for or against whatever the assertion is about, or which expresses such an attitude. For example, in saying "I promise to return this book tomorrow," I commit myself, logically, to a specific future action. In saying, "I commend Jones for his restraint," I imply that I approve of Jones' restraint. In saying, "I look on you as a father," I express an attitude toward you. In each case I *cannot* deny the self-involvement. I cannot deny that "I promise . . ." commits me, or that "I commend . . ." implies a favorable attitude, or that "I look on you as a father" expresses an attitude. The "cannot" is a *logical* one. It is based on part of the *meaning* of the utterance, namely its performative force: what one is doing in saying such-and-such. This meaning or force depends on public linguistic and institutional conventions, though it sometimes also depends on special contexts of meaning or on the special intentions of the speaker (what he means in saying such-and-such).[31]

The distinguishing mark of a self-involving utterance is that saying it commits us and involves us. If I were to say, "I promise to show up at noon tomorrow, but don't count on me to be there," my hearer would be perplexed: The problem arises because this sentence denies part of its own meaning, the self-involving part.

Excepting those "flat constatives," Evans thought that "most language is to some extent expressive," i.e., language that reveals one's feelings.[32] But the exceptions would be those utterances that had no logical self-involvement, such as the utterances of science (although Evans notes that a scientist may be psychologically involved with his theories).[33] Evans makes this distinction hard and fast, arguing that no neutral, scientific utterance entails any utterance that expresses one's feelings and that no neutral statement entails any utterance that is self-involving. So with Evans, we have two basic sorts of language: neutral (scientific) and expressive.

But this dichotomy raises a problem. Are there any utterances that have no self-involvement? Austin could find none. In fact, *all* language (not "most" as Evans claimed) is expressive. Another follower of Austin, John R. Searle, labeled this the *essential* condition for saying anything.[34] Even statements are self-involving on Evans' definition of "self-involving" for if a scientist makes a statement, he is logically committed to defending its truth. If an accountant issues a statement reporting the solvency of some firm, he is logically committed to substantiating his statement if challenged. As with the incoherence of a retracting promise, so with statements: "I hereby state that XYZ and Co., Inc. is solvent, but don't ask me how I know it," said by an accountant, is incoherent and self-contradictory. As Austin's dichotomy between performative and constative broke down, so does Evans' between neutral and expressive language.

Beyond this technical problem, Evans introduces and develops a key notion to ground his understanding of talk of God: *onlook*. He claimed that an onlook fell into Austin's category "behabative," the expression of an attitude. The "necessary and sufficient condition for an attitude is (a) being for or against or (b) regarding as important or unimportant."[35] The typical onlook takes the form, "I look on x as y." As well as expressing attitudes, some onlooks have commissive, autobiographical, behabative or verdictive elements. Which elements an onlook has depends on what sort of onlook is expressed. Some are literal: "I look on Smith as a troublemaker." Some are parabolic: "I look on Henry as a brother, though we are not related by blood." Some are analogical: "I look on music as a language." Some are metaphysical: "I look on human beings as persons (rather than minds or bodies)." The various sorts of onlooks are an important part of our everyday talk, and we regard them as such. "Onlooks are practical, putatively-objective and serious. They are appraised in such terms as profound/superficial, reasonable/unreasonable, true-to-reality/mistaken, adequate/inadequate, coherent/inconsistent."[36] The expression of our attitudes in onlooks is a crucial part of our speaking in general.

One sort of onlook is religious talk of God in that it expresses the speaker's attitude to God and attempts to be objective. But if God-talk is expressive, self-involving and autobiographical, can it also be "true"? How do we account for the claim that belief in God is claimed to be true? In an onlook such as "I look on God as Creator of heaven and earth" we are adopting a stance toward life as a whole in looking on everything (parabolically?) as God's work. Evans suggests that the religious onlook is not only expressive or behabative, but also verdictive—and that there are various assessments of the propriety of the verdict rendered:

> When I adopt a parabolic onlook towards . . . life as a whole, the verdictive element may be interpreted as an *imposition* of meaning or a *discovery* of meaning. Modern existentialist atheism insists on the former; religious belief is the conviction (or hope) that one's onlook conforms to an authoritative onlook, a divine onlook.[37]

But before we can decide which interpretation is correct, we must understand what the speaker means.

To understand a religious onlook, one has to be in rapport with the person who expresses it and one has to share the onlook to some degree. As Evans wrote:

> Understanding depends on rapport; and since it does, my success or failure in understanding an action may provide evidence concerning the sort of person *I* am. . . . The main point I wish to make is this: it is difficult to understand the rationale or intention of an action where the agent is more mature, profound or 'spiritual', or when the agent's action is something which one has not performed oneself (for example, climbing a mountain, painting a picture, or cuddling a baby).[38]

But if rapport is necessary to understand acts, does that include speech acts? Evans' list curiously omits them. But assuming that rapport is necessary to understand speech acts, with whom must there be this rapport? The speaker? If so, why must the rapport be any more than simply understanding the words uttered, as Evans assumes? Or is the agent here the "more spiritual" agent referred to in a verdictive, "I look on God as the Creator of the world"? If the rapport must be with God, Evans assumes what the onlook must argue for: that there is a divine onlook!

The religious onlook includes the conviction that "there exists a hidden Being who has an authoritative onlook."[39] It certainly seems to be true that we are unable to have a profound understanding of God's acts and onlook. But is this because God is a more mature, profound or spiritual agent than we are? Or is it because there is no God with whom to be in rapport? In other words, it seems that we may have some understanding of the religious onlook, but perhaps never a full understanding.

While we may, to some degree, understand a religious onlook, the question arises whether such a view is appropriate, proper or happy. Evans has not offered a clear-cut choice on deciding this question. But it seems that such a question does not even *have* to be decided. The necessary and sufficient conditions for an attitude—and, hence, for an onlook—are "being for or against, or regarding as important or unimportant." It is not part of the conditions for having an onlook that there be any God for it to refer to; one can have an onlook whether or not there is a divine onlook. All that is necessary is that one consider such belief important. But if a person considers it important to have good food, a strange utterance such as "I look on unicorns as delicious eating" fulfills the conditions for being a proper onlook as well as "I look on God as a loving father." Both of these can be understood, but the former seems outrageous, while the latter religious. Unhappily, Evans does not distinguish clearly between these.

And what of opposed onlooks? Consider a profound parabolic onlook such as "I look on God as the possessor of the authoritative onlook." To understand it, we must be in rapport with a speaker of it. But consider an opposed parabolic onlook, such as "I look on God as the projection of men's infantile neuroses." To understand this, we must be in rapport with its speaker. But could someone be in rapport with both? And to assess the conflict between the two must one be in rapport with both? Perhaps a biblical scholar who also was trained as a psychiatrist would be in the proper position to render a verdict. But what of the rest of us? Evans offers us no way to resolve the tension between the claims that each of these on-looks make. In Evans' terms, "flat constatives" or neutral asser-tions do not imply any onlooks. But neither do one's onlooks involve correct statements about what there is. Onlooks do entail verdicts, but it is not clear just how one is to render a proper religious or metaphysical verdict, or how one is to be in position to do so.

Religious talk of God generally deals with attitude-dependent onlooks. The onlook simply presumes that what is looked on exists. But why ought one presume that? All of the following, in different ways, presume that their objects exist. All of them also fulfill Evans' necessary and sufficient conditions for being an onlook, and so are "valid" onlooks:

"I look on those elephants as threats to my life," cried the man in delirium tremens (DT's).

"I look on you as a lover," confessed the beloved.

"I look on God as a loving father," praised the Christian.

"I look on life as an absurd rat race," said the harried sales-man.

In his multiplication of examples, Evans rendered a subtle and sympathetic analysis of the various senses that metaphorical lan-guage might have in various situations, but left the problem of the reference of religious talk of God unsolved.

While one might note that onlooks accurately express the speaker's attitude, successfully induce some effect in a hearer and perform numerous actions, it seems that to discover the reference of language about God, one must have deep "rapport" with the user of that language (or is it with God?). Outside of such rapport, no well-based verdict can be rendered. In other words, unless one has the appropriate attitude, one cannot, logically cannot, be in the proper position to render a verdict about the reference of an onlook. "Neither nature nor Jesus provides an adequate basis for a *self-involving* confession of faith in God the Creator unless they are interpreted in terms of a complex pattern of biblical or quasi-biblical onlooks."[40] It can only be hoped for and presumed that the God who is a loving Father and Creator of heaven and earth exists. The truth of the putative reference of Christian talk of God is impossible to decide from the outside of the Christian community, and from the inside the claim is self-verifying and unquestioned. Evans does not solve the problem of reference, but he does help our understanding of God-talk's meaning. He points up dramatically a necessary condition for the proper, appropriate or happy *utterance* of talk of God: One must have the appropriate attitude. But what the proper attitude or "rapport" for *assessing* the correctness of the reference of talk of God by religious people is remains unanswered on Evans' terms.

More influential in accounts of religious language than the work of Austin has been the work of Wittgenstein. A large number of theorists, most of them critically labeled "Wittgensteinian Fideists" by Kai Nielsen,[41] have been exploring Wittgenstein's significance for the philosophy of religion. Premier among these is Dewi Z. Phillips who continues to publish subtle and provocative elucidations of religious language.

Dewi Z. Phillips

Understanding Phillips must begin with noting key concepts he takes from Wittgenstein. First is the analogy between religious beliefs and pictures. Second is that religion is a "form of life" distinguishable from other "forms of life" by the "language-games" that comprise it. The third is that philosophy neither criticizes nor justifies religion, but rather explicates it.

Phillips' view of religious beliefs as pictures is developed in reaction to Wittgenstein's *Lectures and Conversations on Aesthetics, Psychology, and Religious Belief*. Wittgenstein noted that we often learn the meaning and use of the word "God" by the use of pictures (e.g., Michelangelo's Sistine Chapel ceiling depicting the creation of Adam). Noting that the difference between one who does and one who does not believe in God is like one who does and one who does not believe in a picture, Phillips claims that such belief is not at all like believing in a hypothesis. He writes:

It does not involve the weighing of evidence or reasoning to a conclusion. What it does involve is seeing how the belief regulates a person's life. "Here believing obviously plays much more this role: suppose we said that a certain picture might play the role of constantly admonishing me, or I always think of it. Here an enormous difference would be between those people for whom the picture is constantly in the foreground and the others who don't use it at all."[42]

Either one sees something or one doesn't. Either one is guided by the picture or one is guided by another picture. This claims that religious beliefs are not emotional attitudes (as Ayer and Braithwaite could maintain), nor are they empirical hypotheses (as Flew maintained), but have the status of the background against which hypotheses are verified and attitudes assessed. These beliefs are absolute, "the criteria, not the object of assessment. To construe these beliefs as hypotheses which may or may not be true is to falsify their character."[43]

These pictures are not simply illustrations of something more fundamental. Rather, the picture or view that one has of the world is fundamental to any of the various parts of it, which can only be fully understood in the context of the picture. To learn the meaning of the picture, one learns how to react; and Phillips calls religious beliefs "expressive reactions."[44] And the loss of the meaning of the picture is associated with an inability to react in accordance with it and express one's faith by means of it. Phillips writes:

> The untimely death of one's child renders talk of God's love meaningless for one. One might want to believe, but one simply cannot. This is not because a hypothesis has been assessed or a theory tested, and found wanting. It would be nearer the truth to say that a person cannot bring himself to react in a certain way; he has no use for a certain picture of the situation.[45]

It is not that *something* has changed when one changes (often unwillingly) one's picture; the *whole* is different. To parody a saying of Wittgenstein, "The world of the religious person is a different one from that of the nonreligious person."[46]

The use of certain pictures, the ability to react in certain ways, and the talking of whatever there is in a certain way constitute a "form of life." The religious beliefs specifically are the "language game" that constitutes a form of life. And, as Wittgenstein put it, "What has to be accepted, the given, is—so one could say—*forms of life.*"[47] As there are various ways of living constituted by various ways of reacting to whatever there is, so there are various forms of life. Each has its own language, and each language has its own rules for the correct and proper ways of talking just as each game we play has its own rules. Yet even these languages or language games are not entirely separate from one another. As Phillips has noted in response to critics:

> Having recognized, correctly, that the meaning of religious beliefs is partly dependent on features of human life outside religion, philosophers conclude, wrongly, that one would be contradicting oneself if one claimed to recognize this dependence and also claimed that religious beliefs are distinctive language-games. They are led to this conclusion *only because they assume that the relation between religious beliefs and the non-religious facts is that between what is justified and its justification, or that between a conclusion and its grounds.*[48]

That is, it is not the facts that justify the language games or forms of life, but it is only against the background the forms of life provide that we can understand what the facts are. There is a relation between nonreligious facts and religious responses to what there is, but it is the relationship between the parts of the picture and the whole.

However, the forms of life and the language games that comprise them overlap. There are religious men who are also in science (which seems to be, in Phillips' terms, a form of life different from that of religion). Phillips does not deny this, but simply notes that whatever forms of life exist are not externally justifiable. As sympathetic critic Donald Klinefelter put it:

> His point here is that although religious language-games must necessarily gain significance from aspects of human life which are quite intelligible without reference to religion . . .

nevertheless the force of religious responses to such facts or events cannot be justified in any external way—it can only be *shown*.[49]

This discussion of language games and forms of life as the criteria by which we justify our other beliefs, rather than as beliefs that stand in need of justification, leads to the Wittgensteinian conception of philosophy that Phillips adopts.

Wittgenstein claimed that philosophy was a discipline that left everything as it was, neither providing a foundation for what there is nor an explanation of it. Rather, philosophy attempts to show one the way around what there is by describing how language is used. One application Phillips makes of this is to the concept of prayer:

Wittgenstein's point implies that the meaning of "prayer" is in the activity of praying. The philosopher's trouble comes from the fact that he finds it difficult to give a conceptual account of a familiar religious activity. . . . The conceptual accounts of the believers must be judged on the grounds of whether they accommodate the various features which the "life of prayer" exhibits. The same is true of any philosophical account of prayer. Philosophy does not provide a foundation for prayer, it leaves everything as it is, and tries to give an account of it. . . .[50]

Those philosophers who attempt to understand and criticize faith are doing a task that is at best superfluous and at worst incoherent. Not only does religion not require an explanation; attempting to explain religion in other terms is a misunderstanding of the proper work of philosophy.

To understand talk of God and religions in which such talk plays a constantly important role, one cannot take the position of the neutral spectator. To understand one must be involved, as the following illustrates:

Could a philosopher say that he believed God exists and yet never pray to him, rebel against him, lament the fact that he could no longer pray, aspire to deepen his devotion, seek his will, try to hide from him, or fear and tremble before him? In short, could a man believe that God exists without his life being touched at all by the belief?[51]

If he could, then would such a philosopher be talking at all of the God in whom religious people believe and of whom they speak? Talk of God is part of the religious form of life; it is a crucial part of the language used in that form of life. But to extract that part of the language from the language game and to examine it *in vitro* instead of *in vivo* changes the meaning of that part that has been extracted. To talk about "God" outside of the form of life in which belief in God is fundamental has no implications for the meaning of "God" within the form of life:

> All one can say is that people *do* respond in this way. Many who respond in one way will find the other responses shallow, trivial, fantastic, meaningless, or even evil. . . . But philosophy is neither for nor against religious beliefs. After it has sought to clarify the grammar of such beliefs its work is over. As a result of such clarification, someone may see dimly that religious beliefs are not what he had taken them to be. He may stop objecting to them even, though he does not believe in them. Someone else may find that now he is able to believe. Another person may hate religion more than he did before the philosophical clarification. The results are unpredictable. In any case, they are not the business of philosophy.[52]

Philosophy is not the explainer or examiner, but merely the clarifier and elucidator that lets the chips fall where they may.

Phillips' great contribution for understanding talk of God is noting that it is part and parcel of a way of life. But could it not be the case that all the believers are held captive by a picture that is simply wrong? Wittgenstein himself, in discussing the work of the logical positivists—including himself—wrote: "A *picture* held us captive. And we could not get outside it, for it lay in our language and language seemed to repeat it to us inexorably."[53] Wittgenstein managed to place that picture in the context of a larger one that he developed later. But could the same be true of talk of God? In Phillips' account, there is no way at all for us to discover that our "picture" might be wrong! Even though it is not likely, even though we believe it to be true, even though it holds us captive, in a pluralistic world it is a real possibility that the believer must consider: Our picture may be wrong. In an age in which there are others whose lives are happy and full "using other pictures," how can we consider ours completely unquestionable or infallible?

In chapter five we will turn to Phillips' views again on the justification of talk of God, so the full story has not yet been told here. But the full story has also not been told for Phillips is still working on his position and it may be the case that he will solve some of the problems mentioned here in his later works.

Conclusion

In this chapter the problems of discovering the sense and reference of talk of God have been approached from two classic positions and three modern ones. Although the discussion has been rather critical, it has also been appreciative. Can we draw any general conclusions now? I think that there are two.

First, the attempt to set off religious talk generally or talk of God in particular as a *unique* way of talking, a way radically different from other human ways of speaking and communicating, is a mistake. In different ways, Evans, Phillips and Zuurdeeg tend to do this. The result of this sort of strategy is that the skeptic is left in possession of the field. He can claim that the believer has been unable to justify his use of the word "God" and has retreated from an important human battle into the citadel of faith. If talk of God is not in any way reasonably defensible and explainable to non-believers, how can the believer persuade the non-believer of the goodness, utility or truth of his position? How can the skeptic undermine a person's faith? Such does happen; any account of talk of God that does not show how this can occur can be considered explanatorily inadequate.

Second, awareness of the researches of modern empirical

philosophy does not totally vitiate the positions taken by forebears such as Aquinas and Arnold. But Austin's theories and Wittgenstein's investigations show that the work done by earlier thinkers is not complex and subtle enough to account for the various work language in general and talk of God in particular can do. So what we have need of is a theory that lays out clearly the similarities and differences of talk of God and other sorts of talk. We need a theory aware of modern philosophy of language. We need a theory that accounts for the manifold meanings of religious talk of God and the success or failure of its intended reference. Finally, we need a theory that can show how it is possible to account for and adjudicate the reasonable differences between believers and unbelievers. In the next two chapters, we shall examine theories that attempt to do this work adequately.

Notes

1. Numerous positions have been taken during the last hundred years or so over just what Thomas intended to say, just what his writings meant, and just how he is to be understood properly today. His doctrine of analogy that underpins his whole theology has been under careful scrutiny and the object of much theological debate. David Burrell, *Analogy and Philosophical Language* (New Haven: Yale University Press, 1973) has an excellent chapter on Aquinas that cites much of the recent discussion about his theory of analogy. Burrell's complex work yields a modified and qualified support of a Thomistic doctrine of analogy. Humphrey Palmer, *Analogy: A Study of Qualification and Argument in Theology* (London: Macmillan and New York: St. Martin's Press, 1973) has claimed that the doctrine of analogy does no real work and, finally, ought to be discarded, suggesting that neither a reformed doctrine of analogy nor Thomas's theory gets us anywhere. Those interested in pursuing the doctrine of analogy are invited to attend to these texts and the sources cited in them.

2. Cf. A. C. Pegis, ed., *The Basic Writings of St. Thomas Aquinas* (New York: Random House, 1945), pp. 112-13.

3. *Ibid.*, p. 118.

4. *Ibid.*, p. 120.

5. *Ibid.*, pp. 126-27.

6. *Ibid.*, p. 131. In checking the Latin text, I used an edition of the *Summa Theologica* published by the Dominicans (New York: McGraw-Hill, 1964). Their English translation is much freer than that of Pegis. Numerous suggestions for the best translation of *esse ipsum* have been suggested. Pegis uses "being itself"; the Dominicans use "existence it-

self"; and David Burrell has suggested that "ground of being" may be of use (*Analogy and Philosophical Language*, p. 128).

7. Burrell, *Analogy and Philosophical Language*, p. 122.

8. David Hume, *Dialogues Concerning Natural Religion*, ed. N. K. Smith (New York: Bobbs Merrill [Library of Liberal Arts], n.d.), pp. 130-87.

9. Burrell, *Analogy and Philosophical Language*, p. 127.

10. Matthew Arnold, *Literature and Dogma: An Essay Towards a Better Apprehension of the Bible* (New York: Macmillan, 1898 [First edition, 1873]), pp. 5-6.

11. *Ibid.*, pp. 10-11.

12. *Ibid.*, p. 16.

13. *Ibid.*, p. 18.

14. *Ibid.*, p. 70.

15. *Ibid.*, pp. 97-98.

16. *Ibid.*, pp. 194-95. Compare 242-48.

17. *Ibid.*, p. 264.

18. *Ibid.*, p. 304.

19. *Ibid.*, p. 305.

20. *Ibid.*, p. 348.

21. R. B. Braithwaite, *An Empiricist's View of the Nature of Religious Belief*, reprinted in *Christian Ethics and Contemporary Philosophy*, ed. I. T. Ramsey (London: SCM Press, 1966), p. 69.

22. Willem F. Zuurdeeg, *An Analytical Philosophy of Religion* (Nashville: Abingdon Press, 1958), p. 59.

23. *Ibid.*, p. 26.

24. *Ibid.*, p. 27.

25. *Ibid.*, p. 57. Zuurdeeg often seems to misunderstand the thrust of empirical philosophers. For instance, he suggests that philosophical analysis is ordinary language's "meta-language" (that language which explains the grounds for and limits of ordinary language) and that both of these conform to logic. But then since convictional language may be illogical, logical analysis won't be able to fathom convictional language. Convictional language does not have the same logic or form as ordinary language, but it does have *a* logic, which the empiricists would say Zuurdeeg is attempting to explore. Zuurdeeg's misapprehension of the various meanings of "logic" mars his own work, as do other terminological mistakes that he makes.

26. *Ibid.*, p. 59.

27. *Ibid.*, p. 193; emphasis added.

28. *Ibid.*, p. 32.

29. John L. Austin, *How To Do Things With Words*, ed. J. O. Urmson (New York: Oxford University Press, 1970 [First published, 1962]).

30. *Ibid.*, pp. 150-51.

31. Donald D. Evans, "Differences Between Scientific and Religious Assertions," in *Science and Religion: New Perspectives on the Dialogue*,

ed. Ian G. Barbour (New York: Harper and Row, 1968), p. 112.

32. Donald D. Evans, *The Logic of Self-Involvement* (London: SCM Press, 1963), p. 79; also see pp. 108f.

33. For further discussion of this point, see Evans, "Differences Between Scientific and Religious Assertions," pp. 113f.

34. John Searle, *Speech Acts: An Essay in the Philosophy of Language* (New York: Cambridge University Press, 1969), pp. 66-67. Searle's understanding and use of Austin's work differs considerably from Evans' but a comparison and contrast would contribute little to understanding the strengths and weaknesses of Evans' work for the purposes of this exposition.

35. Evans, *The Logic of Self-Involvement*, p. 124.

36. *Ibid.*, p. 128.

37. *Ibid.*, pp. 139-40.

38. *Ibid.*, pp. 111, 113.

39. *Ibid.*, p. 255.

40. *Ibid.*, p. 267.

41. See Nielsen's article, "Wittgensteinian Fideism," *Philosophy* 62 (July 1967).

42. Dewi Z. Phillips, "Religious Beliefs and Language Games," in *Faith and Philosophical Enquiry* (London: Routledge and Kegan Paul, 1970), p. 89. He quotes Ludwig Wittgenstein, *Lectures and Conversations on Aesthetics, Psychology, and Religious Belief* (Oxford: Basil Blackwell and Berkeley: University of California Press, 1966), p. 56.

43. *Ibid.*, pp. 90-91.

44. Dewi Z. Phillips, "Infinite Approximation," *Journal of the American Academy of Religion* 43, 3 (September 1976): 486.

45. Phillips, "Religious Beliefs and Language Games," p. 100.

46. Cp. Ludwig Wittgenstein, *Tractatus Logico-Philosophicus*, trans. D. F. Pears and B. F. McGuiness (London: Routledge and Kegan Paul, 1961 [First German edition, 1921]), § 6.43: "The world of the happy man is a different one from that of the unhappy man."

47. Ludwig Wittgenstein, *Philosophical Investigations*, trans. G. E. M. Anscombe, 3rd ed. (New York: Macmillan, 1968 [First Edition, 1953]), p. 226.

48. Phillips, "Religious Beliefs and Language Games," p. 101.

49. Donald S. Klinefelter, "D. Z. Phillips as Philosopher of Religion," *Journal of the American Academy of Religion* 42, 2 (June 1974): 322. I have been usefully guided by Klinefelter's article and Herbert Burhenn, "Religious Beliefs as Pictures," in the same number.

50. Dewi Z. Phillips, *The Concept of Prayer* (London: Routledge and Kegan Paul, 1965), pp. 8, 10.

51. Phillips, "Faith, Scepticism and Religious Understanding," in *Faith and Philosophical Enquiry*, p. 14.

52. Phillips, "Religious Beliefs and Language Games," pp. 108-09.

53. Wittgenstein, *Philosophical Investigations*, § 115.

4
Personalist Empiricists

In this chapter two theorists who find that talk of God has many senses and a definite reference will be considered. Both are influenced strongly by recent work in philosophy, especially that of Wittgenstein and his philosophical followers. Both are empiricists, but "broad" empiricists who recognize that there are more facts than scientific facts, more values than emotional values, more truths than simple truths. However, their differences are many, although their positions may not be totally incompatible. Both have weaknesses in their work, but these are relatively minor in the light of their strengths. The first theorist to be considered in this chapter is Dallas M. High, an American philosopher of religion, who was trained at Duke University and teaches now at the University of Kentucky.

Dallas M. High

The basic understanding of religious uses of language that informs High's theory is drawn from the work of Wittgenstein in a manner rather different from that of D. Z. Phillips. Central to High's work is the importance of understanding the users of language as well as the uses that can be made of language. In his major effort to date on God-talk and religious language generally, *Language, Persons and Belief*,[1] and in subsequent articles exploring some themes in understanding how people do talk of God or other religious subjects,[2] High's continuing concern is to show that any analysis of any sort of language that ignores the speaking person is inadequate.

Although he has been lumped among the "Wittgensteinian

71

Fideists" by one critic of conceptual relativism,[3] High does not belong in that category. His interpretation and use of Wittgenstein's work differs markedly from that of Phillips and the other post-Wittgensteinian philosophers of religion. High emphasizes the overriding importance of the person who speaks and opposes those "attempts . . . to contract the actor, 'I', out of speech even when it obtains implicitly."[4] Any attempt to analyze language of any sort apart from the user is doomed to inadequacy. I, as a person who speaks, am involved in many forms of life; my language follows the rules of many language games; my personal backing is necessary for what I say to have meaning. Ignoring the personal involvement that is part of the situation in which meaning and comprehension occurs is an unhappy abstracting and analyzing of "dead marks and scratches and sometimes residuals of waste matter."[5]

High's analysis of the sense and reference of talk of God depends on some notions he takes from Wittgenstein. The first of these is the notion that the meaning of a sentence can sometimes (but not always) be identified with the way it is used. "Words and sentences in themselves are neither meaningful nor meaningless. They attain these characteristics only by virtue of having something done with them."[6] Thus to understand the sense of "I believe in God the Father, the Almighty, the maker of heaven and earth," we must understand what the speaker is doing in saying those words. If he is merely reciting an old poem, or practicing lines in a play, or mocking what Christians do, then this sentence has meanings different from the "same" sentence when Christian believers confess their faith using those words. The declaimer, the actor, the satirist and the believer each do different things with the same words in different situations. Although the words are the same, the meaning in each situation is different. And the same person finds himself in many different situations with the need to do different things with the same words—and to find just what some words mean we need to see just what some writer or speaker did with them or is doing with them and in what situation he speaks or writes. High explains this and draws his implications as follows:

> To appeal to the "use" of language for the understanding and recovery of the meaning of our language, is to appeal to the

ordinary linguistic activities of human life in their multiple but mixed forms. What these activities *are* is shown by the way people think and live as ways of being in the world.[7]

To understand the meaning of a sentence is to understand how *people* actually use the sentence; to understand how it is possible to use the sentence is to understand how it is possible for the sentence to mean something.

The ways in which we use our sentences—whether about God or anything else—are understandable on an analogy with games: Just as we play many games with many different sets of rules, so we engage in many linguistic performances each with its own set of rules to guide us in the proper way of proceeding. In the rules of baseball, I cannot score a field goal; but in basketball I can (if I follow all the rules *and* get the ball in the hoop) score a field goal and make two points; and in football I can (if I follow all the rules *and* kick the ball between the uprights above the crossbar) score a field goal and make three points. The rules to be followed and the acts to be performed depend on which game one is playing; the rules to be followed and the acts to be performed in using one's words depend on which language game one is playing. And, like other sorts of games, language games have overlapping rules and terminology. Language games also overlap in that a single person may play *many* games. These overlaps are crucial, for otherwise one might think that these games were completely different from each other. High writes:

> Here we run the danger of making different language-games appear as neatly separated compartments of discourse which are mutually exclusive of one another such as to say, as is sometimes said, for example, "Literature and philosophy are totally different language-games." Wittgenstein's intention to show us differences and to illustrate the "multiplicity of language-games" is not an open invitation to seal off various kinds of speech from one another.[8]

The claim High makes amounts to understanding that any theologian who believes that the language of religion is totally unique and separate from other uses of language is self-deceived.[9]

The most important difference between High's understanding of Wittgenstein and Phillips' understanding of Wittgenstein becomes obvious in discussion of the concept "form of life." Whereas Phillips seems to understand each language game as informing a given form of life, High understands each form of life as consisting of a number of language games. The basic point in Wittgenstein's work is this:

> It is easy to imagine a language consisting only of orders and reports in battle.—Or a language consisting only of questions and expressions for answering yes and no. And innumerable others.—And to imagine a language means to imagine a form of life.[10]

High's discussion of "form of life" underlines the close relationship between language and life, but implicitly denies the correctness of identifying a form of life as constituting and being constituted by a language game.

> The notion is fully positive since it is our "form of life" which provides the sense and sensibility of our speech. Therefore, to deny or attempt to escape these forms, which is to deny or attempt to escape human life itself, not only brings philosophy to grief, as Wittgenstein argued, but assaults language and breeds a perverse kind of sensibility. . . . Wittgenstein is reminding us that words, symbols, and sentences, woven together with action, finally rest upon the concept of human life in all its social, cultural, or interpersonal forms. Likewise, what we understand and count as reality (or the world) is closely connected with the language and human life, particularly our conceptual forms.[11]

What is basic, according to High, is human life. However, just what a form of life is—according to Wittgenstein, High or Phillips—is not very clear. They all agree: "What has to be accepted, the given, is—so one could say—*forms of life*."[12] But is science a form of life? Or Western culture? Or middle-western farm life? Or college dormitory residing? Or religion in general? Or each religion in particular? On Wittgenstein's terms, ambiguous as they are, we don't know. High opts for "Western culture," with many language games, as a form of life. Phillips opts for a particular picture of or expressive reaction to the world as determining a form of life—but this, too, is a problem, for it is unclear just how much we must agree on the details of a picture to be said to share the "same" picture. While neither conclusively establishes his understanding as the correct one (a task that might be impossible and certainly is difficult), High's has the virtue of being more inclusive and more easily defended.

In the context of these Wittgenstein-inspired reflections, High notes that the sense of any utterance—including talk of God—comes from the actual ways in which people can use language. High writes:

> These manifold and heterogeneous ways of speaking have their meaning not in the words themselves (they alone have no "life") but in the way people "use" them. There is no single-track way ("picture," "reference," or whatever) in which a word can be said to mean, just as there are no constitutional guarantees it will mean except as people "get it" or place some confidence in each other's speaking.[13]

High contends that our words have their meaning from the sense that we give to them; apart from our understanding of them—and of each other—there is no understanding the sense of our talk.

One of the ways that we talk is to express our beliefs. Two important aspects of this appear in High's work. First, while beliefs may be examinable independent of someone's believing them, this is an abstraction from the act of believing. "Believing is something *performed, owned,* and *claimed by, for* someone, *about* and *in* someone or something."[14] What is primary on High's account is not *beliefs* but *believing*—not what is believed, but the person who believes. Both can be subject to scrutiny, examination and clarification, but an impersonal scrutiny is not sufficient, for the primary element—the believing person—is ignored. Second, this is related to a curious aspect of believing noted by Wittgenstein: "One can mistrust one's own senses, but not one's own belief. If there were a verb meaning 'to believe falsely,' it would not have any significant first-person present indicative."[15] The point here is that I can say that *he* believes falsely, but I cannot say that *I* believe falsely. Any attempt to do so yields utter nonsense.

The implications of this analysis of the peculiarity of the first-person present indicative active (singular or plural—a point High neglects) shed much light on the falsification controversy and the non-cognitivist and fideist accounts of religious language:

> Some have even gone so far as to equate the test procedures of third person factual truth conditions with the meaning. Therefore, the objector who claims that belief utterances must specify their descriptive or factual truth conditions in order to be meaningful is barking up the wrong tree. This does not mean that belief utterances are immune from or cannot claim a home in the same logical environment as "reason," "giving reasons," "rational," "rationale," and "responsibility." Equally wrongheaded are those theologians who retreat into the "confessional" circle of paradox, irrationality, and theological immunity. They commit the egregious blunder of accepting the third-person model of the conditions of meaningful belief utterances. Hence, they find it necessary to cloak themselves in the robes of unduly necessary dogmatism.[16]

To believe in God—and to say "I believe in God"—is not to believe that some facts are true. It is more than that; it is to place trust in another person or Person. To say that I believe in you does not mean that I believe some facts about you; rather it means that I trust you and that trust has something to do with, but is not limited to, the "facts" about you. Similarly, to believe in God means that I trust God and that trust has something to do with, but is not limited to the "facts" about God (or the world).

The attempt to understand this sort of belief-in as an inference from facts makes the mistake of construing third-person factual utterances as primary. High writes:

> Just as my recognition (or knowledge) of *you* as a person having privileged particular identity is not a straightforward

inference from the behavior of bodies (although my thinking and talking about *your* personhood will *include* thinking and talking about *your* actions and body), so too God is not picked out or said to exist by inference (logical or empirical) from the world (although, again, thinking and talking about *God* will include thinking and talking about His actions and world).[17]

Our whole way of talking of other people presumes that they are persons, not automata. Our whole way of talking about God and the world cannot be based on the presumption of atheism, but on the presumption that there is something to be talked of, trusted in and worshiped. We can no more prove the existence of God than we can prove the existence of ourselves.

Hence, the sense of a believer's expression of his belief in God is rather complex. It has to do with the stance he takes, what he sees in the world, what he has been taught and how his fellows understand him. Talk of God has many senses, many meanings, dependent on who the believer is, what he says, and the context in which he says his belief. For this talk of God to be fully justified, it must refer to a God that actually exists. But how are we to know that some talk of God does so?

What we attempt to do, High says, is to justify, give reasons for, and to anchor our beliefs. We have many—good and bad —reasons for believing in God. Yet what would count as a decisive account or reason for the presumption of theism and talk of God? There can be none: "Given the human condition of speaking and reasoning, neither evidence-for (verification) nor evidence against (falsification) is a conclusive evidence or guarantee, even though both are useful and used."[18] There are no necessary or sufficient reasons for believing that can be determined from a neutral, detached, third-person, point of view. As High writes:

The range and possibilities are indeed open-ended. To ask specifically for the "reasons" and "justification" is to launch an inquiry, a quite historical one, into what *people* do give and have given as "reasons" and "justification." "What *people* accept as a justification—is shown by how they think and live." Such is an inquiry into life and culture itself. Yet, again, this is not an inquiry that relieves *us* of *personal* claims

and ownership, nor does it relieve *us* of all doubt, suspicion
and risk. But this is not a weakness; it is precisely the character of "believing," "thinking," "reasoning," "speaking," and
"life" itself as we know it and must accept it if *we* are to say
anything at all, let alone say anything intelligently. Religious
believing shares in this human adventure.[19]

The sense of talk of God is what *we* make of it. The reference of talk
of God is to the Creator of heaven and earth; but whether such
reference is justified is an "open question" upon which each believer takes a stand—even though that stand cannot be fully justified.

The virtue of High's work, clearly, is that it notices that there
are many senses for talk of God and many ways for justifying that
talk. However, there are weaknesses, too. The problem of deciding what "form of life" means and how it is related to "language
games" plagues High's thought—and it seems clear that his is not
the majority position in the interpretation of Wittgenstein's work.
High takes Wittgenstein in a direction that would be approved of
by those who accept the work of John L. Austin, but not approved
of by those who would not accept Austin's work.[20] Finally, a
generalized vagueness pervades High's work: What is a person?
This is High's crucial term, and nowhere do we find an analysis of
what it means to partake in the human condition. Hints occur in his
work, but none of these go far to establish a "philosophical an-
thropology." To leave one's most crucial term so unspecified is a
major weakness.

Besides the above problems, no further major work has appeared from High's pen since *Language, Persons and Belief* in
1967. Clearly the historical investigation he talks of (above) is a
necessity to flesh out his basic theory. We need guides to see what
has, does (and ought to?) count as "good reason" and "justification" even though these will not be sufficient guides for our own
believing. Until such work appears, we may recognize High's work
as an interesting beginning, but an adventure whose continuing
story needs to be written. While it is well and good to maintain the
priority of persons, his approval of the following seems to leave the
person as speaker totally without guides: "As a medical professor

put it to me, 'A patient is dead when I say he is dead.' That was not meant as arbitrary, but as reasoned and responsible. 'But,' he added, 'it is difficult to teach that, and it cannot be learned by a set of rules or principles.' "[21] We still need to see what *is* the difference between arbitrary and responsible, both in finding a person dead and in expressing belief in God. Until High specifies this crucial difference somehow, we must find his work important, but incomplete.

If High's work in the field has been scanty, that of Ian T. Ramsey, onetime scholarship student at Cambridge, later chaplain and tutor in Christ's College, Cambridge, subsequently fellow of Oriel College and Nolloth Professor of the Philosophy of the Christian Religion in Oxford, and finally the Anglican bishop of Durham, England, from 1966 until his death in 1972, has not only been voluminous, but scattered throughout many books, journals and *festschriften*. The balance of this chapter will be devoted to the second theorist who finds that talk of God has many senses and (at least) intends to make a definite reference when it is used properly.

Ian T. Ramsey

As with Dallas High, the concept of the self plays an important role in the thought of Ian Ramsey. The role, however, is somewhat different. Although Ramsey's account of the self is a bit scanty, understanding it is necessary for understanding his central contention that " 'I' will never cease to be a useful guide when we are confronted with puzzles about 'God.' "[22]

Although he had been deeply influenced by idealist philosophy at Cambridge, Ramsey's move to Oxford coincided with a change in theological style that accounted for, was influenced by and went beyond the conceptions and critiques of empirical philosophers. In talking about the self, Ramsey claimed that Hume's bundle-theory of the self, which claimed that my "self" is nothing but a bundle of impressions that happen to be bound together, was inadequate. Because Hume could find no distinct impression of the self, he allowed that any "self" or "soul" was an illusion. Following Berkeley, however, Ramsey argued that some words could function significantly in spite of the fact that they did not correspond to impressions. One of these words was "I," which Ramsey showed to be rather elusive. Although "I" was not factually describable, publicly observable or completely analyzable in terms of the plain facts, it nonetheless could be allowed to be significant.[23] The reason that "I" could function significantly was not due to the memory of self-awareness, but rather the discernment of a pattern disclosed in the actions and events of one's life. The metaphor Ramsey used to illustrate this contention was that of the center of a circle, although other examples could be used. My life, my self, my character is not simply a bundle of events, but a pattern of actions. Although the facts that are the events are needed to understand who I am (what the shape of the bundle is), no single fact nor all of them together is sufficient to understand who I am. Who I am systematically eludes all descriptions, although those descriptions can indicate the shape of my character or self.

Later Ramsey claimed that the notion of the self that he developed had a certain content:

All this suggests that the one unifying concept, definitive of personality, is not soul nor mind nor body. There is no kind of underlying cushion to which all our bodily and mental events and characteristics are attached as pins; and any basic personality matrix is not static. Rather is personality to be analysed in terms of a distinctive activity, distinctive in being owned, localized, personalized. The unity of personality on this view is to be found in the integrating activity . . . expressed, embodied and scientifically understood in terms of its genetic, bio-chemical and endocrine, electronic, neurological and psychological manifestations. What we call human behaviour is an expression of that effective, integrating activity which is peculiarly and distinctively ourselves.[24]

To talk of a human person one could describe the events of his life, the acts he had done and the shape of his character. All of these are necessary, but not sufficient to describe the actor, the "I" who I am.

In his journey from idealism to empiricism, Ramsey moved

from a discussion of a timeless self to a self in time.[25] That self cannot be described scientifically, although it is possible to discern a pattern of actions through which an awareness of the self, of the character of the individual, can be disclosed, induced or evoked. Ramsey took Hume's bundle-theory and turned it on its head. Each event or action of a life *may* be understood alone, but to do so does not satisfactorily explain the "feeling" or "intuition" of self-awareness or subjectivity that even Hume admitted.[26] Ramsey explained that feeling not on the basis of some privatistic theory, nor on the grounds of some incorrigible intuition, but on the basis of a checkable, evaluable intuition or feeling. That is, the feeling of continuity and self-conscious awareness is based in the awareness of the *character* of one's life; the content of that notional awareness is based in and disclosed through the set of actions and events that form one's life; and the understanding can be modified or corrected by improving one's knowledge of the events and the pattern they form in one's life. The only way we can finally speak of what a self or "I" is, is in metaphors or models that reveal—but do not describe—who we are.

Talk of God parallels talk of who I am. First, it must be grounded in a situation in which one has a vision, intuition or feeling of the whole universe through the ordinary facts and features of the situation and take the form of an ultimate claim. Or, as Ramsey put it, all talk of God must be grounded in a "cosmic disclosure."[27] Ramsey characterized the development of talk of God from this sort of experience as follows:

A cosmic disclosure is a situation which has come alive both subjectively and objectively, where a "plain", "flat" situation restricted to the data of sense experience has taken on "depth" or, as we say, "a new dimension". As the situation takes on depth objectively so I, as subject, take on depth subjectively; I too come alive. . . . There is no supernatural separated by a gulf from the natural, but a supernatural of fulfilment, not denial. Further, the objectivity of God is in the last resort safeguarded as being grounded in that which is *other than myself* in such a cosmic disclosure, where I am aware of an activity meeting my own. In so far as I am aware of being relatively passive, of being acted upon, to that degree I am aware of what confronts me which is other than myself, and it is this which in a fully developed conceptual scheme can be called "god". Such a conceptual scheme arises from interweaving with an eye to comprehension, consistency, coherence and simplicity, the various strands of discourse to which various models, central to cosmic disclosures, give rise.[28]

This informal characterization of his position includes not only the philosophical components that contribute to his account of talk of God, but also psychological components to illustrate his theory. But his point is clear: The reference of talk of God is guaranteed —it is that which we encounter in a cosmic disclosure situation. But the problem remains to be solved: What sense, if any, does talk grounded in a cosmic disclosure have, and does it refer successfully?

When a situation of cosmic disclosure occurs, the response of the individual is of discernment *and* commitment. But specifically religious commitment "combines the 'depth' of personal or quasi-personal loyalty . . . with the [unlimited] range of mathematical and scientific devotion."[29] Religious discernment "sees" the more-than-the-ordinary in the ordinary, "understands" facts beyond the plain facts. Both discernment and commitment are necessary for the religious person: "Such a commitment without any discernment is bigotry and idolatry; to have the discernment without an appropriate commitment . . . is insincerity and hypocrisy."[30] The language, then, that we use to talk of what we have seen (discernment) and what we have felt (commitment) must express both in such a way that neither is reduced to ordinary commitment/discernment. Yet, to be understandable, this language must be related to everyday language. The way that this was to be done was by what Ramsey called qualified models.

Qualified models are the proper use of talk of God. A model is a tool for understanding whatever is disclosed to us. Ramsey, following Max Black, identified two different sorts of models: picture models and disclosure models. The first type is theologically uninteresting. It simply attempts to "reproduce, in a relatively manipulable or accessible embodiment, selected features of the 'original.' "[31] The disclosure model differs from the picture model in that the disclosure model has the more "abstract aim of reproducing the *structure* of the original," rather than reproducing a "scale model" of the original. The function of the disclosure model is slightly different as well. It is intended to generate further insight, to evoke new disclosures. It can do this because it does not attempt to be a sufficient picture of what is disclosed, but an evocative representation of the "original." Ramsey's examples of disclosure models included the structural formulae of chemistry and the human nervous system modeled as a computer and the examples of scale models included a child's toy train. Qualified models are, then, a sort of disclosure model. But what sort?

The pivotal point of distinguishing theological from scientific disclosure models was proposed in the context of their similarity! Ramsey wrote:

> It is my thesis, then, that by virtue of the models they employ, or the distinctions native to their exercise, *all disciplines* combine insight and discursive reasoning, mystery and understanding.[32]

The discipline of theology is not an exception. However, the *emphasis* in theology was different: on the insight disclosed, rather than on the reasoning; on the mystery to be understood, rather than on the understanding. The theological emphasis is accentuated by the use of qualifiers that form part of theological models. Qualifiers are words (or phrases or prefixes) that are directives to use the model until a characteristically different situation—a cosmic disclosure situation—occurs.[33] While the models themselves are representative, the qualifiers are prescriptive, intended to show that the "original" the models represent (God or the ultimate) cannot be pictured, described or understood completely.

Ramsey used and discovered numerous qualifiers to generate his theological models. Most, if not all, were derived from traditional Christian theology. Donald Evans organized these qualifiers into three sets: universalizing, perfecting and negating. Universalizing qualifiers (the "all" in almighty, the "omni" in omniscient) function to instruct the user of the model (the "mighty" in al-mighty, the "knowing" in omniscient) to extend "the range of observables in space and time so that the descriptive term [the model] has all-inclusive scope and hence a new meaning."[34] Perfecting qualifiers—usually the word "infinitely"—instruct one not to expand the *range* of events that the model represents, but rather the *quality, intensity* or relative *perfection* of the model.[35] Consider, as an example of this, the following:

Billy loved his sister enough to give her his lollipop (some love).
John loved Jean enough to give her his kidney (a lot of love).
Ned loved Sue enough to give her his whole life (more love).
Dag loved humanity enough to serve people all his life (even more).

Yet God so loved the world (cosmos) that he gave his only-begotten Son (Jn. 3:16) (an intense, unlimited love).

Here, the model (love) is developed in the first four examples, where we see an increase in the intensity of love. But the fifth example is qualified in such a way that it is *not* simply the highest in a series. Rather, this is a love without limits in either range or scope, an understanding of which is to be gained only by evoking a situation characteristically different from those that preceded it. The analogy Ramsey used was an attempt to see a circle as a regular polygon with an infinite number of sides. The qualifier "infinite" tells us "not to be content, but to specify a regular polygon with at least one side more" until the "light dawned" and we "saw" a circle.[36] And just as the word "circle" is odd from the point of view of "polygon language," so too will the word "God"—and the talk of God's infinite love—be odd from the point of view of "everyday language."

While perfecting and universalizing qualifiers tend to overlap, negating qualifiers, such as the prefixes "im-" or "in-" attached to models such as "mutable" and "passible," seem different. Evans described their use concisely:

We are directed to start with the models, fixing on mutable or passible features of perceptual situations, and then to apply the qualifier "not", progressively obliterating these features.

The words "immutable" and "impassible" are not descriptions of God; rather, they are designed "to give a kind of technique for meditation", so as to "bring about that discernment which is the basis for talking about God."[37]

Yet some qualifiers work as both negating and universalizing, depending on how they are used. "Eternal" and "necessary" can be construed both as "including all time" and "presupposition of everything," or as "non-temporal" and "non-contingent."[38] Finally, models for God also might qualify each other by jostling each other: calling God a "fortress," a "rock and shield," a "father" and a "power that makes for righteousness" means that none of them are adequate by themselves. Ramsey described this method of qualifying models as follows:

> Mystery is now safeguarded by recognizing that to talk adequately of the God who is disclosed on any occasion will need language culled from and growing out of all the models which arise in all the vast variety of circumstances in which God has been disclosed. . . . This is a rather more rough and ready way of qualifying: by the jostling of models. Here is another less orderly, and more haphazard way of being articulate about a mystery.[39]

Of course, this haphazard method of qualification had special pitfalls. As Ramsey argued in numerous places, Christians have often gotten lost in tangles of theological discourse drawn from many models, and the task now is not to be *more* articulate about God and his acts for mankind, but to be *less* verbose about a mystery.[40]

Generally, Ramsey considered qualified models to be disclosure models. With other disclosure models they must incorporate a structural similarity between themselves and the phenomena they represent, yet must not picture what they represent; they must arise in moments of disclosure. Theological models differ from other disclosure models in that they must arise in a situation of *cosmic* disclosure, where what is disclosed is discerned as unlimited; they are to be judged in terms of how stable they are over a wide range of phenomena and a long period of time rather than in terms of how many verifiable deductions can be made from them; properly, they are to be qualified to emphasize the mystery and transcendence of that which is disclosed in a cosmic disclosure and that of which they speak. They are "acceptable, persuasive, clear and so reliable guides to what at the present baffles us."[41]

In Ramsey's view, qualified models do five sorts of things, i.e., they have five senses or uses. First, they *refer* to the Other encountered in a situation of cosmic disclosure, an Other that Christians address as God. If they do not so refer, then they are empty. Second, they *represent* the Other through the use of models drawn for everyday discourse. But they also, third, *indicate*, through the use of qualifiers, that the word "God" stands outside of or beyond everyday talk. Implicitly, they also indicate that God is more than, but related to, the everyday world. Fourth, qualified models function to *evoke* disclosures. Ramsey clearly believed that such a pattern as the one on page 84 above could enable another to see—discern and be committed to—God. The better that a model did evoke disclosures, the better it was. Fifth, qualified models *generate stories and license discourse* based on them. The stories that we tell of God's mighty acts may be generated by reflection on qualified models and must be related to them; if our talk is *not* related to qualified models, then we have no way of showing that it is in any way about God, for we are engaging in unlicensed discourse.

But even "properly" licensed talk, based on qualified models, can go wrong. Ramsey illustrated this in a discussion of the doctrine of hell.[42] In this discussion he made two major points: first, that discussions about what properly can be *said* about God are discussions not of God but of our sayings! Ramsey wrote:

> Let us realize that we shall never be in a position to talk about God's intentions, and that in any case it is not what God can or cannot do, but rather what we can or cannot say about him. Recalling . . . Augustine: in all this we do *not* judge God, but only our understandings of, our discourse about God.[43]

Second, that the peripheral images—such as hell as a place of fire and brimstone with sinners eternally weeping and gnashing their teeth—are simply that: *peripheral*. To treat them as central obscures what is truly central: God.

> To put it very crudely, most parables and most apocalyptic need reading backwards, back into the disclosure of God which is at their heart and centre. Once we recognise in this way the *imaginative* logic of eschatology and the parables, the great . . . difficulties of a doctrine of Hell completely disappear, and we also see where, and where not God comes in.[44]

And any "religious" talk that cannot lead us to God is bogus. If we allow our talk to get away from its proper determining center, then we are, to say the least, walking on precarious ground. The stories we generate always must be tied back into the model that licensed it and the model is our way of talking about God. If such a road cannot be found, we ought to quit telling such stories.

Ramsey wanted theology and preaching to weed out bogus talk and to confine itself to proper sorts of talk. But let us assume that we follow his rules. Let us say that we do, indeed, confine our talk about God to qualified models and our other religious talk to stories that illustrate our understanding of God and to our proper worship of God. What is the result of this? Ramsey claimed that we could be *sure* of God, while remaining *tentative* in our theology:

> My point then is that we are to be tentative, but always contextually tentative, about our theology, while grounding that theology in a disclosure of God. In this way we are to be sure in religion while being . . . tentative in theology. This means that at each stage, the tentative is controlled by the context to date, so that we always assert something firmly and squarely in a context. But such assertions are always ripe for development. This development must link any new asser-tion ever more coherently with the Creeds and Scriptures, and lead us to a greater comprehensiveness in so far as that new assertion will presumably match up better to a variety of contemporary challenges. So to be justly tentative in theol-ogy is to build continuously on an ever-changing context of

pro tem. certainty and to have the humility which, while it strives energetically to build from such a base the best theological map it can, recognizes that it will *never* succeed in "embodying" the Mystery. A contextually tentative theology is not a euphemism for scepticism; nor does it suppose that all theologies are equally good; nor is it an excuse for sloth and ignorance. It is rather an apt counterpart to our vision of God. . . . We are learning better to be as frank with friends as with opponents, and to be as charitable to opponents as to friends.[45]

But such a humble and beautiful conception of talk of God also has its problems. For how are we to know that it is of *God* we are talking, rather than something else?

Depending on the precise meaning of that question, Ramsey offered three answers. One, the general theory for the justification of talk of God, will be considered in the next chapter. But two other answers remain to be discussed. The first has to do with the similarities of the words "God" and "I." The second details Ramsey's justification for believing in a personal God.

In one sense, we can be as sure of God as we are of ourselves. How do I understand who I am? On Ramsey's terms, I must use models (e.g., husband, father, teacher, philosopher) and theories (e.g., models of humans as constituted by chemicals, influenced by stimuli, etc.) to understand clearly that intuition of who I am. How do I understand who God is? I must use models and talk derived from models to explain to myself and to others the notion of what I have met in a cosmic-disclosure situation. Just as my self-understanding can change, so can my understanding of God change. Just as I may be (but am convinced that I am not) wrong about myself, so I may be (but am convinced that I am not) wrong about God. Just as my appreciation of what my activity entails may change, so my appreciation of what God's activity is and entails may change. Just as I realize who I am by understanding how I act, so can I realize who God is by acknowledging his mighty acts. The formal similarity of talk of God to talk of I means that we can be as sure of what or who God is as we can be sure of what or who I am.

Yet many would find this sort of formal similarity unsatisfactory. In fact, philosopher of religion Ninian Smart found it so unsatisfactory that he claimed that Ramsey was a virtual atheist who did no more than give the name "god" to a group of experiences in which we felt that the "penny dropped" or the "ice broke."[46] Ramsey responded vigorously to Smart's charge detailing the ways in which Smart had misunderstood the import of his work.[47] Ramsey also wrote an essay, "A Personal God," that defended his conviction that there is a God properly characterizable as "personal":

> My argument is, then, that we may speak of God as "personal", we may attribute "personality" to God, if there occur, whether deliberately generated or not, cosmic situations of a disclosure kind whose patterns are isomorphous with disclosures of personal reciprocity.[48]

If cosmic disclosures are seen as similar to those disclosures we have of other persons as living and active agents who interact with us, then we can attribute "personality" to God. But while this may legitimate one's attitude toward the universe, it seems to say nothing about the universe. Ramsey asked rhetorically, "Am I indeed committed to such a personalistic atheism?"[49] His answer to this question hinges on the notion of *activity:*

> What is logically most primitive about persons is their characteristic *activity* which cannot be reduced to the behaviour they display. A person is distinguished from a machine or from an official, both of whom may be "active" but in no disclosure sense, by the kind of characteristic *activity* he displays in a situation of mutual self-disclosure. When the Universe comes alive in a cosmic disclosure whose structure is modelled by a personal reciprocity, it declares itself to us as a person does; and as a characterization of the *activity* which we then know, "person" is the most natural model of any to use.[50]

If an other which one encounters displays such activity that it evokes a "coming to oneself," then it is reasonable—even natural, as Ramsey says—to construe that other as a person.

This does not exclude the possibility of being mistaken on

some particular occasion. But the possibility of being mistaken
depends upon the possibility of being correct! Ramsey wrote:

> That very possibility, that very distinction between "person"
> and (say) a reciprocally active machine, between "genuine
> person" and paste-board imitation determines that *some*
> cases will be genuine. In the case of God, however, I think
> there is a more direct certainty. For here there is a *cosmic*
> —infinite, all-inclusive—disclosure; and I do not see on
> what grounds there could be the kind of mistake possible in
> [mistaking a clever machine for a person]; for I do not see on
> what grounds we could deny the "otherness"—the confront-
> ing activity, or even posit a variety of referents rather than a
> single individuation.[51]

Although we encounter *many* persons, we live in and encounter
one world; and if one of those encounters (or many of them) is a
cosmic disclosure characterizable as "personal," or reciprocally
"active," then we can say naturally that what we encountered was
"personal."

This argument places much of the burden of justifying our
belief in a personal God on the validity of "religious experience." Is
the "activity" that he claimed is encountered in the situations of
cosmic disclosure the same as or analogous to the "activity" met in
situations of personal disclosure? Ramsey clearly thought that the
term "activity" was not analogous but univocal here, and that the
criterion of one's *response* to the encounter was sufficient if these
responses to cosmic disclosures could be shown to be non-
illusory.

The argument he offered for the non-illusory character of
these experiences was that just as a personal response to a real
person underlies personal response to a fake person, so personal
response to a real personal God underlies personal response to a
fake god, i.e., to our projections, or hopes, or our delusions. But
just as a response to a fake person is dependent upon the possibility
of responding to a genuine person, so the response to a fake god
depends upon the possibility of response to a genuine God. Thus
finally construing all cosmic disclosures as responses to fake gods

is precluded since response to a fake god depends upon the response to a real one.

This argument falters in that it assumes what is at issue: whether there *is* anything to respond to in responding to God. But it shows that Ramsey is persuaded that *persons* (rather than bodies or minds) are primary; analogously, the world-as-a-whole (rather than events or objects) is primary. As persons are not bundles of events but centers of activity, so the world is not a bundle of events but the arena of activity where God and persons meet and interact. Neither the facts and features of the world nor those of one's character are primary; they are derived from what is primary. And the claim is that as far as one's response to part of what one encounters in this world as a person is justified, so far is one's response to the whole of what one encounters justified, *if both evoke a personal response*. Of course, we can be mistaken. Sometimes one may respond to part of the whole as if it were the whole, to something impersonal as if it were personal. But if one does respond to the whole in a cosmic disclosure as if it were a person, that response is as justified as a response to a person.

Ramsey's argument is the reversal of what C. B. Daly attributed to modern positivism: The most meaningful (because most real) are God and selves.[52] A theory that stops short of the personal (subjectively) or the world-as-a-whole (objectively) is inadequate. Such a theory leaves out the primary, the most important and the most meaningful. It ignores the disclosure of my self in the events of my history and the disclosure of God in the events of the history of the universe. Conceiving this God as personal is as legitimate as conceiving my self and other individuals as personal. Without this sort of completion a history is incomplete for it deals only with abstractions. Ramsey's argument for a personal God shows that there are good grounds for believing in a personal God, meets the charge that he was a virtual atheist and brings out the force of his fundamental claim that we can be sure of God, but must be tentative in our theology.

While Ramsey's theory of the senses and reference of talk of God is the most comprehensive yet provided, that does not mean that it is flawless or final. It relies on a certain sort of religious experience, and, as John Hick notes, "Any special event or experience which can be construed as manifesting the divine can also be construed in other ways."[53] It is based on a plausible, though not inescapable, view of what it means to be a person. It presumes that, in a very literal sense, there is *one* world, a claim that is also plausible, but not inescapable. Finally it drives a wedge between talk of God and experience of God. While some do not find this a problem, others would want to discover a link between religious experience and religious language stronger than Ramsey's.

Conclusion

The theorists considered in this chapter both construe persons as primary, although what each does with this presumption is different. Dallas High and Ian Ramsey have presented relatively adequate theories of talk of God. Both have found that talking of God has many senses and that it refers to a Being (or Being-Itself or ground of Being or Power-not-ourselves, depending on which model of God's mode of existence one believes to be most satisfactory) that can reasonably be called "God." While High's work is sketchy and Ramsey's was scattered, both offer points of view that account for believers' talk of God in such a way that a reflective and aware Christian could recognize the picture they paint as being a portrait of what believers do when they talk of God.

One final question remains to be discussed. The problem of justifying our talk of God, while not absent from the work of any of the theorists considered in these four chapters, has become a focus of much debate in philosophy of religion done in an empirical mode. The major theories of the justification of religious language (generally) and talk of God (specifically) are the subject of chapter five.

Notes

1. Dallas M. High, *Language, Persons and Belief* (New York: Oxford University Press, 1967).

2. Dallas M. High, "Morality of Speaking," *Lexington Theological Quarterly* 5 (July 1970): 64-75; "Belief, Falsification and Wittgenstein,"

International Journal for Philosophy of Religion 3 (Winter 1972): 240-50; "Death: Its Conceptual Elusiveness," *Soundings* 55 (Winter 1972): 438-58. High also edited a collection of articles by other thinkers, *New Essays on Religious Language* (New York: Oxford University Press, 1969).

3. See Roger Trigg, *Reason and Commitment* (Cambridge: Cambridge University Press, 1973), p. 65.

4. High, "Morality of Speaking," p. 72.

5. High, *Language, Persons and Belief*, p. 22.

6. *Ibid.*, p. 67.

7. *Ibid.*, p. 69; emphasis added.

8. *Ibid.*, p. 75.

9. *Ibid.*, p. 87.

10. Ludwig Wittgenstein, *Philosophical Investigations*, 3rd ed., trans. G. E. M. Anscombe (New York: Macmillan, 1968) § 19.

11. High, *Language, Persons and Belief*, p. 101.

12. Wittgenstein, *Philosophical Investigations*, p. 226.

13. High, *Language, Persons and Belief*, pp. 135-36.

14. *Ibid.*, p. 160.

15. *Ibid.*, citing Wittgenstein, *Philosophical Investigations*, p. 190.

16. *Ibid.*, pp. 161-62.

17. *Ibid.*, pp. 181-82.

18. *Ibid.*, p. 211.

19. *Ibid.*, p. 212; emphasis added. High quoted Wittgenstein, *Philosophical Investigations*, § 325.

20. See Garth Hallett's review of *Language, Persons and Belief* in *Theological Studies* 29: 150-52. Compare the discussion of Austin in the context of Evans' work in chapter three above for work done explicitly in that vein. For a clear presentation of Austin's work at greater length, see J. W. McClendon and J. M. Smith, *Understanding Religious Convictions* (Notre Dame: University of Notre Dame Press, 1975), chapter three.

21. High, "Death: Its Conceptual Elusiveness," p. 456.

22. Ian T. Ramsey, *Religious Language: An Empirical Placing of Theological Phrases* (London: SCM Press, 1957; New York: Macmillan, 1963), p. 43 in the later edition.

23. See Ramsey, "The Systematic Elusiveness of 'I,'" *Philosophical Quarterly* 5, 20 (July 1955) and "Biology and Personality: Some Philosophical Reflections," *Biology and Personality*, ed. I. T. Ramsey (Oxford: Basil Blackwell, 1965); both reprinted in *Christian Empiricism*, ed. J. H. Gill (London: Sheldon Press; Grand Rapids: Eerdmans, 1974).

24. Ian Ramsey, "Human Personality," in *Personality and Science*, ed. I. T. Ramsey and Ruth Porter (London: Churchill Livingstone, 1971), pp. 127-28.

25. Even a superficial reading of Ramsey, "Man and Religion: Individual and Community," *Library of the Tenth International Congress of Philosophy*, Volume I: *Proceedings of the Congress* (Amsterdam: North Hollands Publishing Co., 1949), pp. 424-26, in comparison to "Human Personality," *op. cit.*, will show this.

26. David Hume, *A Treatise of Human Nature*, ed. L. A. Selby-Bigge (Oxford: Clarendon Press, 1955), pp. 635-36.

27. For example, Ramsey, *Christian Discourse: Some Logical Explorations* (London: Oxford University Press, 1965), p. 79, and in other places throughout his works.

28. Ian Ramsey, "Theology Today and Spirituality Today," *Spirituality Today*, ed. Eric James (London: SCM Press, 1968), pp. 82-83.

29. Ramsey, *Religious Language*, p. 39.

30. *Ibid.*, p. 19.

31. Ian Ramsey, *Models and Mystery* (London: Oxford University Press, 1964), p. 3. Ramsey refers to Max Black, *Models and Metaphors: Studies in Language and Philosophy* (Ithaca: Cornell University Press, 1962), especially pp. 221-22.

32. *Ibid.*, p. 56; emphasis added.

33. Compare Ramsey, *Religious Language*, p. 70.

34. Donald D. Evans, "Ian Ramsey on Talk About God," *Religious Studies* 7 (1971): 218.

35. *Ibid.*

36. Ramsey, *Religious Language*, p. 77. Dewi Z. Phillips has criticized this sort of attempt to ground talk of God in "Infinite Approximation," *Journal of the American Academy of Religion*, 44, 3 (September 1976): 477-87.

37. Evans, "Ian Ramsey . . . ," p. 218; see Ramsey, *Religious Language*, p. 60.

38. *Ibid.*, pp. 222-23.

39. Ian Ramsey, "On Understanding Mystery," *The Chicago Theological Seminary Register* 53, 5 (May 1963): 10. Another illustration of the method is seen in "Talking About God: Models, Ancient and Modern," in *Myth and Symbol*, ed. F. W. Dillistone (London: S.P.C.K., 1966). Both have been reprinted in *Christian Empiricism*.

40. See, for example, *Religious Language*, chapter three; *Christian Discourse*, chapter two; *On Being Sure in Religion* (London: Athlone Press, 1963); and "Hell," *Talk of God*: Royal Institute of Philosophy Lectures II (London: Macmillan and New York: St. Martin's, 1969), pp. 207-25.

41. Ramsey, *On Being Sure in Religion*, p. 18.

42. Ramsey discussed the doctrine of hell in "Hell" and in *On Being Sure in Religion*, but the exposition is much clearer in the former.

43. Ramsey, "Hell," p. 215.

44. *Ibid.*, p. 221; emphasis added.

45. Ramsey, *On Being Sure in Religion*, p. 90.

46. Ninian Smart, "The Intellectual Crisis of British Christianity," *Theology* 158 (January 1965): 31-58; reprinted in *Christian Empiricism*. There is also a follow-up letter in the July number, pp. 351-52.

47. Ian Ramsey, Letter to the editor, "The Intellectual Crisis of British Christianity," *Theology* 158 (February 1965); reprinted in *Christian Empiricism*.

48. Ian Ramsey, "A Personal God," in *Prospect for Theology: Essays in Honour of H. H. Farmer*, ed. F. G. Healey (London: Nisbet and Co., 1967), p. 65.

49. *Ibid.*, p. 66.

50. *Ibid.*; emphasis added.

51. *Ibid.*, p. 68.

52. C. B. Daly, "Metaphysics and the Limits of Language," in *Prospect for Metaphysics*, ed. I. T. Ramsey (London: Allen and Unwin, 1961), pp. 178-205.

53. John Hick, *The Philosophy of Religion*, 2nd ed. (Englewood Cliffs: Prentice Hall, Inc., 1973), p. 30.

5
How To Justify
Talking of God

The previous chapters have discussed the various theories offered in the empirical tradition to account for the sense and reference of talking of God. This chapter envisions a precise focus on one crucial problem involved in talking about God: How can such talk be justified? Granted that reasonable and good people have found talk of God not only meaningless but positively pernicious, how can their challenge be met by those who do talk of God even after the "death of God"?

Of course, the justification problem has hardly been absent from our previous discussions. David Hume claimed that talk of God could in no way be justified. A. J. Ayer and Antony Flew, for different reasons, agreed with Hume's conclusion. Yet even on grounds allowed to be in some sense meaningful (though not *cognitively* meaningful) by the narrow empiricists, the non-cognitivist analysts attempted to justify talking of God on the grounds that religious talk does something else besides tell the empirical truth. So the apparent defeat of theism at the hands of the tough-minded was really a victory that allowed the non-cognitivists to see the *real* meaning of religious language. Or so they claimed.

A more intriguing approach has been the claim that some religious language, but specifically Christian talk of God, could be verified eschatologically. The basic idea has been attributed to Ian Crombie.[1] However it has been John Hick who, as professor of philosophy at Cornell and Princeton Theological Seminary, lecturer in divinity at Cambridge, and now professor of theology at the University of Birmingham, has explicated and defended the notion of eschatological verification.

John Hick

According to the logical positivists a statement could not be meaningful unless it could be verified. Hence, to be meaningful, theological claims that express religious faith "must make an experienceable difference whether they are true or false."[2] Something must happen that makes it clear that a claim is either true or false: This is the essence of verification.

Yet on the surface of it, there seems to be no experiential difference in the world for the theist or the atheist. We all live in the same partly good, partly bad, world; we are all on the same path that ends in death; we are all going to have the same experiences whether or not there is a God. But what of the end of that path? The theist and the atheist may disagree not about the details of their journey, but only about its end. "And yet when they do turn the last corner it will be apparent that one of them has been right all the time and the other wrong."[3] Indeed, the issue between them, Hick claims, is a real issue, not an illusory or meaningless one, in spite of the fact that there may not be any experiential difference here and now.

Hick summarizes the intent and the importance of the notion of eschatological verification neatly:

> Christian doctrine postulates an ultimate unambiguous state of existence *in patria* as well as our present ambiguous existence *in via*. There is a state of having arrived as well as a state of journeying, an eternal heavenly life as well as an earthly pilgrimage. The alleged future experience of this state cannot, of course, be appealed to as evidence for theism as a present interpretation of our experience; but it does suffice to render the choice between theism and atheism a real and not merely empty or verbal choice. And although this does not affect the logic of the situation, it should be added that the alternative interpretations are more than theoretical in that they render different practical plans and policies appropriate now.[4]

It is this crucial, factual, yet ultimate difference that, in Hick's view, defeats Hume's claim that the dispute between the theist and

the atheist is merely verbal, Ayer's claim that theological beliefs
are meaningless because unverifiable and Flew's contention that
talk of God is meaningless because unfalsifiable.

However, it must be noted that the work Hick intends the
notion of eschatological verification to do is very limited. First, it
does not "confirm" a believer in his faith, but answers the philosophical inquiries concerning which "aspects of Christian belief
bring that system of belief within the accepted criteria of factual
meaningfulness."[5] Eschatological verification is not present verification for either the believer or the unbeliever; it solves no present
problems. Second, eschatological verification does not set out the
complete conditions necessary for affirming or denying the truth of
the claim that God exists. Such a task would involve a complete
definition of the nature of God, a task usually claimed to be impossible by Christians. Rather, eschatological verification shows that
the claim that God exists is a factual claim, i.e., one that can be
assessed in true-false terms. It shows that "the concept of deity, in
its Christian context, involves eschatological expectations which
will be either fulfilled or not fulfilled."[6] Eschatological verification
tests the truth of "God exists," but it does not define the full
meaning of "God exists." Third, eschatological verification does
not treat "the existence of God as a metaphysical hypothesis which
hopes for confirmation in the future."[7] Faith in God is not
"hypothetical." Hick concludes that the notion of eschatological
verification has one very precise use:

> Its relevance is rather to the issue of the logical status of
> theistic language; for it brings out a feature of the concept of
> God which establishes that the claim to be conscious of the
> divine presence [here and now] is not merely the expression
> of an idiosyncratic "slant" upon the world, but involves an
> assertion which is factually true or false because it is, if true,
> subject to verification within *future human experience*.[8]

But is this one precise use, one relevance, any use at all?

In the end, Hick's theory of eschatological verification does
not do much work. First, from the side of those inclined to believe
that God exists, it offers no practical help. Hick concedes this. But

it also takes as the standard for understanding what utterances are assessable in reasonable terms (rather than unreasonable or emotional ones) the claim of the verificationists, a claim that is rather dubious, as we noted in chapter one. While it certainly is the case that some critics of Christian faith hold to a strict verificationism, the arguments, on the whole, have become much more involved and much more subtle. As seen with Donald Evans and Dallas High, almost every religious utterance has some representative value as well as emotional involvement; so would be the case with almost every antireligious utterance. In the end, the believer has to acknowledge that the notion of eschatological verification offers no help when he or she is confronted *today* by a person of genuine good will and intellectual acuity who challenges faith in God.

From the side of the skeptics, second, there are some real problems involved in the conception of eschatological verification. To say that some proposition, theory, hypothesis or assertion (*p*) has been verified is "to say that (at least) someone has verified it, often with the implication that his or their report to this effect is generally accepted."[9] But to say that someone has verified *p* entails that it was possible for someone to verify *p*. While Hick shows through the use of a tortured example that eschatological verification is a logical possibility,[10] the question remains whether it is a credible possibility, if in actuality such an experience *will* occur for some person. It is a *logical* possibility that 250 years from now I will be able to verify the winner of the Indianapolis 500 auto race in the year 2007. But a *credible* possibility? Hardly, for it assumes that I will be around to verify (and probably to be able to state) a fact when I am 280 years old! Hick simply presumes that there will be some "future human experience" that will, at least for some, verify the proposition that God exists. But why should I assume that *if I am a skeptic*? While I may concede that there is such a logical possibility, I may not concede that such a possibility has the slightest chance of being an actual occurrence. Eschatological verification, by ignoring those situations in which the quest for justification of one's religious faith in God arises, offers us no help in understanding how we can justify here and now a faith in God. The skeptic confronting the believer, holding different views on what human experience is and can be and arguing with the believer, raises the problems of the meaning and truth of belief in and talk of God. While eschatological verification may, if the theory is successful, succeed in establishing that the argument is (at least in part) over matters factual, it is profoundly unsatisfying in that it offers no way to adjudicate that factual dispute here and now.

If Hick's development of a theory taken from a major reaction to the "Theology and Falsification" discussion has not offered a satisfactory way of talking about the justification of talk of God, that does not mean that nothing useful has emerged from the discussion. In fact, one of the participants in the discussion has since developed his thought to the point of publishing *The Justification of Religious Beliefs*. Basil Mitchell, fellow of Oriel College and Nolloth Professor of the Philosophy of Religion in Oxford, has attempted to offer an account of justification of talk of God and it is to that account that we can now turn.

Basil Mitchell

Mitchell begins his work by noting that neither proofs nor disproofs of the existence of God seem to work or to be convincing.[11] But if this is the case, have the "proofs" any use at all in the attempt to justify one's belief in God? Mitchell's basic answer follows:

> What has been taken to be a series of failures when treated as attempts at purely deductive or inductive argument could well be better understood as contributions to a cumulative case. On this view the theist is urging that traditional Christian theism makes better sense of all the evidence available than does any alternative on offer, and the atheist is contesting the claim. The dispute concerns what Gilbert Ryle calls "the plausibility of theories" rather than proof or probability in any strict sense.[12]

The argument for Christian faith in God is not an attempt at a hard-and-fast proof, but rather an attempt to account for whatever there is, as well as possible, and a claim that (overall) Christian theism works best to do so.

In order to understand how to adjudicate the cumulative cases made for and against theism, Mitchell turns to an analogy with the philosophy of science. In *The Structure of Scientific Revolutions* Thomas S. Kuhn describes what happens when an overriding vision of the world is overthrown by another vision that proposes a new "normal" way of proceeding or a new "basic paradigm" on which science is to model itself:

> At times of revolution, when the normal-scientific tradition changes, the scientist's perception of his environment must be re-educated—in some familiar situations he must learn to see a new gestalt. After he has done so the world of his research will seem, here and there, incommensurable with the one he had inhabited before. That is another reason why schools guided by different paradigms are always slightly at cross purposes.[13]

Mitchell notes that "the process of transition from one paradigm to another is not strictly a change in interpretation, since there are in such a case no fixed data for the scientist to interpret."[14] But what happens during the time of a scientific revolution? How can one choose which side is most deserving of one's support, commitment and allegiance? Ought one to fight for the "old ways" or to proselytize for the "new"? If an individual cannot understand the other perspective fully from within his own and if (by definition) there is no over-arching conceptual framework within which the evaluation can take place, can such a choice be in any sense rational? This is the problem that Kuhn's account of scientific revolution leaves for the scientist—and the philosopher of science—unsolved.

Mitchell finds that there is a remarkable similarity in theological argument. The theist sees problems that need to be explained, where the atheist sees no problems at all. As a scientist of one school might not admit that the problems or evidence of another school make any sense, so might the theist need to explain why the universe is ordered as it is and the atheist see no need for explanation at all. The transition from one school of science to another is remarkably like a religious conversion in which the whole of one's world seems to shift. Mitchell cites Kuhn's discussion to show this:

To make the transition [from Newton's universe] to Einstein's universe, the whole conceptual web whose strands are space, time, matter, force, and so on, had to be shifted and laid down again on nature whole. Only men who had together undergone or failed to undergo that transformation would be able to discover precisely what they agreed or disagreed about. Communication across the revolutionary divide is inevitably partial.[15]

Additionally, the sorts of accounts scientists give of such shifts in their own world views are similar to those given by people who have undergone religious conversions.

Granted that there is a remarkable similarity between the "whole" view of the religious person, which to challenge successfully means to overturn, and the "whole" view of the scientist, is there some way to choose between scientific paradigms that can be an analogy to choosing religious paradigms? Mitchell attempts to show, contrary to the work of some philosophers of science (and perhaps contrary to the claims of Kuhn himself) that the choice between paradigms may be reasonable, if reasonableness and rationality are understood broadly. But if rationality entails following the precise rules of antecedently established conventions (as many would claim), then rationality will not get us far in deciding which paradigm to support, for the heart of the dispute is often just what rules are rational and just what facts there are to be discovered by working in light of these rules.

Mitchell's basic criteria, using a "broadened idea" of rationality, are summarized as follows:

Where there is conflict between two or more scientific paradigms, (a) each can give an account of all the experimental evidence, (b) which of the paradigms gives a better account is something which has to be determined by the judgement of scientists, (c) it is not possible to specify precise rules in accordance with which such decisions are to be made; scientists have to rely on such "values" (to use Kuhn's word) as consistency, coherence, simplicity, elegance, explanatory power, fertility, (d) these criteria are not themselves relative to particular paradigms. Hence, (e) there is no reason to doubt that the choices made with care and competence on the basis of them are rational. And the same may be said *mutatis mutandis* of world-views or metaphysical systems.[16]

Mitchell then applies similar criteria to the disputes between theists and atheists. He assumes that there are important differences between religious and other sorts of judgments. He implies that these differences are formally specifiable in terms of what the beliefs are about. Religious faith has God or the numinous for its object, while the atheist has no obvious object for his ultimate beliefs other than "this worldly" objects. Hence, the political, moral and aesthetic beliefs of an atheist to which religious faith *seems* analogous are really *not* so—because each has a different sort of reference. It is this formal difference between theistic and atheistic beliefs that explains why there are some remarkable differences—and perhaps incommensurable ones—between the "whole view" of the atheist and the "whole view" of the theist.

However, problems arise with Mitchell's attempt to give the rules for judging between competing world views. First, Mitchell is unable to account for "mystic atheists" or for "natural theists." Neither the faith of someone who simply finds this world as-is awe-inspiring nor that of the person who finds God to be a noticeable part of this natural world fits the distinction he draws between theists and atheists. As with Willem F. Zuurdeeg, the attempt to distinguish faith or convictions by their objects is a task doomed to failure. Second, the values themselves may not be paradigm-dependent, but the judgments that find whether or not some scheme or hypothesis or conviction displays a given value will be based on the paradigm with which one is operating. While you and I may agree that elegance is preferable to awkwardness, this is simply because all these values are vague. When it comes to deciding whether some given conception is elegant, if two careful choices be made about them and the choices differ, then both choices—though opposing—would each be rational. This seems to leave Mitchell, in the end, with the real possibility that there are a plurality of rationalities—which raises the question again of how we are to decide among them. Even Mitchell's imprecise rules do not get us out of a vicious circle that seems to have us deciding on the basis of "habit, caprice or inclination." Perhaps it is this problem that Mitchell intends when he talks about the "perpetual possibility of tension between faith and reason."[17] But it seems that the final choice of paradigms—whether scientific, religious, or a-religious—cannot be fully rational.

Certainly there is something right about noting that conversion "from one system to another is rarely effected by rational argument alone, as it involves the believer's entire personality and his whole way of perceiving and responding to the world."[18] But what non-circular role can rationality play in such a choice? In view of such problems the response is often to claim that no outside criteria are either necessary or sufficient to judge whether any talk of God can be justified. It is such a position that D. Z. Phillips takes, and explicit discussion of his view of the problem of justifying talk of God is our next task.

Dewi Z. Phillips

The discussion of Phillips' work in chapter three concentrated on Phillips' understanding of the sense and reference for religious talk of God. Now we need to account for how it is possible, in Phillips' view, to justify talking of God. His central contention in discussing justification follows:

> The philosopher's task is not to attempt to verify or falsify what he sees for that makes no sense in this context. His task is a descriptive one; he gives an account of the use of language involved. He can only say that these language games are played.[19]

Neither the allegedly neutral philosopher (such as Flew), nor the explaining psychologist (such as Freud), nor the descriptive sociologist (such as Emile Durkheim), nor the reductionist theologian (such as Braithwaite) can give an account of religious language because his own preconceptions prohibits each from seeing its full meaning and thus giving a complete account. They tend to mistake one sort of language for another. The language of religion is not philosophy, psychology, sociology, nor even theology. Religious language is religious language and cannot be reduced without remainder to something else:

> Philosophers, anthropologists, and psychoanalysts, in seeking explanations of religious belief, have often regarded such beliefs as fictions, which, in being rendered intelligible, are reduced to non-religious terms. What we have seen, however, is that in this sense of explanation, religious beliefs are *irreducible*. If one asks what they say, the answer we have argued for is that *they say themselves*. One may be interested in investigating the consequences of various religious beliefs for other social movements and institutions, or the historical development of religious beliefs. Yet, such investigations would not be an investigation into the impressiveness of the beliefs. Their impressiveness may be elucidated . . . but it cannot be explained.[20]

But the question remains, just what are religious beliefs saying and how can they be elucidated?

Phillips' answer to those questions is based in work that Wittgenstein did in reaction to G. E. Moore's defense of common sense and that was published posthumously as *On Certainty*.[21] Moore had argued that there are certain propositions that are indubitable, e.g., in response to the philosophers' claim that there are no material things, Moore would respond that they are certainly wrong by showing them two material things: his right hand and his left hand, both of which he knew to exist. Religious beliefs, according to Phillips, share some characteristics with Moore's certainties. First, they seem to be bedrock: "These beliefs are taught not as beliefs which require further reasons to justify them. They are not opinions or hypotheses."[22] Similarly, faith in God is bedrock. The believer neither learns to need nor requires support for his faith. Second, it seems that to contradict a religious belief, one cuts oneself off from a way of talking, rather than disagreeing within a way of talking. If I deny the existence of material objects, then I can say nothing about them—I "cut myself off from" material-object language. If I deny the existence of God, then I can say nothing about him—I cut myself off from God-talk.

There are also differences between Moore's certainties and religious beliefs. If I attempt to deny that I have two hands, I am either mad or a philosopher, but in either event I have cut myself off from ordinary reason. However, if I deny the existence of God, while I cut myself off from talking of God and from religious faith, I do not necessarily cut myself off from ordinary reason. If I do stop talking of God, I have alternatives, e.g., secular atheism. This is not the case with some of Moore's certainties; the only alternative to them is nonsense. Phillips discusses the availability of the alternatives to religious belief in God:

> These are genuine alternatives since they indicate that the person has no use for the religious belief, that it means nothing to him, that he does not live by such a belief, or that he holds other beliefs which exclude religious faith. In this latter case, however, the alternatives are not alternatives within the same mode of discourse, but rather, different perspectives on life.[23]

So far the elucidation of religious beliefs shows that the theist and the atheist are disagreeing with each other, but not within the same mode of discourse or form of life. What they are disagreeing about is whether one or another form of life is preferable.

What happens if one moves from one form of life to another is conversion, an experience or process in which every part of one's life seems turned around, caused by something other than oneself. As an example of conversion, see the sorts of things St. Paul had to say about his (Gal. 1:12) and what Luke had to say about Paul's conversion (Acts 9:1-19; 22:5-16; 26:12-20). And since one's whole life is involved in a conversion either to or from faith, it seems that Phillips is right in claiming: "To ask whether God exists is not to ask a theoretical question. If it is to mean anything at all, it is to wonder about praising and praying; it is to wonder whether there is anything in all that."[24] To ask whether God exists is to ask a question about a form of life; to affirm or deny the existence of God is to decide on participation in or abstention from a way of living and the language associated with it. Hence, Phillips can say:

> "There is a God", though it appears to be in the indicative mood, is an expression of faith. One of its most characteristic forms is showing forth praise. "There is no God" also appears to be in the indicative mood. But it is in fact a denial; it may indicate one of a number of possible negative relations in which a man may stand to the affirmation of faith.[25]

Phillips then concludes his discussion of the question of the existence of God by saying, "The worst misunderstanding is to think that this question is a theoretical one. Not far behind is the belief that philosophers should be able to answer it."[26]

Generally, Phillips rejects theoretical theism and theoretical atheism, "both of which are attempts at philosophizing which will not stand up to examination."[27] Most of the theories discussed in this book are confused for they attempt to give theoretical accounts of talk of God. Both atheists and theists are confused if they try to argue for their faiths. Phillips writes:

> What is confused on both sides is treating "There is a God" and "There is no God" as statements of fact, as *conclusions which result from some kind of finding out*. It is also confused to think that the issues between religious belief and atheism can be settled by some kind of philosophical demonstration.[28]

Hence, we must have religion without explanation, for no explanation is possible, but only exploration and description.

It is extremely difficult to say just what is wrong with Phillips' work, unless one rejects it as a whole, as itself totally confused. It is easy to say what is right with it: Phillips is clearly right in making the believers' understanding of what they say primary; in acknowledging the nonhypothetical status of faith in God and the associated claim that talk of God is not an expression of a hypothesis; in ferreting out the errors of Hume and his successors in philosophy and the social sciences; in elucidating a moving, proper and appropriate attitude toward the dead, especially among Christians; in noting how use of a mode of discourse involves one in a form of life; and in offering a new angle of vision on the chronic debates between theists and atheists. Yet three major confusions flaw Phillips' work.

Phillips claims that metaphysical statements are essentially confused: "Metaphysics goes too far; it is an attempt to say what cannot be said."[29] Metaphysics is more like superstition or neurosis than it is like religious faith. Yet a religious expression that affirms the existence of God is not nonsense in the context of faith, while the same expression with the same reference *cannot* have any meaning as part of a metaphysical statement. In that context, talk of God is nonsense. But why is talk of God's existence apart from religious faith nonsense? While one may not agree with him, it is hard to believe that *all* an atheist metaphysician such as Bertrand Russell had to say about God's existence was nonsense. Further, is all metaphysics (or, better, are all metaphysicians) confused? There are many modes of doing metaphysics, and to say that they all share one defining characteristic—confusion about what *can* be said—is doubtful. To claim that Plato, Aristotle, Aquinas, Hegel, Bradley and Collingwood—to name only a few metaphysicians each of whose positions is rather different from the others'—are all confused needs substantiation. Phillips' anti-metaphysical and anti-theistic-metaphysical claims go too far!

Phillips claims that the utterance "There is a God" ought really be read "God! ALLELUIA!!!" But are the indicative and imperative moods so completely separated from each other? If there is no God to praise, my praise may be totally sincere, but will be misdirected. If I thank my wife for being faithful to me during an absence, my thanks will be sincere—but misplaced if she has taken a paramour; and both of them would be titillated by my blunder. Generally, in every imperative there is implied some indicative claim. This can be seen by looking at English grammar, where the present and future indicative and the hortatory subjunctive can substitute for the imperative:

"Praise God!" (imperative).

"Now we praise God in song" (present indicative).

"We shall praise God" (future indicative).

"Let us praise God" (hortatory subjunctive).

No matter which mood applies, praise to a nonexistent God is misdirected, while praise to an eternal God is appropriate. Until these matters are sorted out and the relation of the "indicative" and "imperative" elements clarified, Phillips' work has problems that need to be solved.

Phillips also mistakenly equates statements of fact with conclusions that result from finding out. As Moore claimed, one knows or is certain of some facts and it is odd to ask how one knows or why one is certain. The oddity arises for they are expressions of facts, but not of conclusions. There are more facts than the scientific, more facts than those we conclude to be true. Some are apparent upon simple examination. Is it possible that the claim that God exists, while not being a conclusion, may entail the fact that God is? Just as the thanking an unfaithful wife for being faithful is flawed, so the thanking of an absent God for his presence is flawed. If the delusion is even worse—thanking a non-existent wife for being faithful or thanking a non-existent God for his loving kindness—it is worse in both cases, sadder in both, crazier in both. While I may have no doubts about my wife or my God, that does not mean that I am not wrong. And it is just these real worries —worries of part of the religious consciousness of many whom William James would label "twice-born"[30]—that Phillips' theories cannot account for.

What we need are accounts that acknowledge both the imperative and the indicative elements (as Phillips might label them) in talk of God. We need to justify, in the face of friends who think we are deluded in our belief in God, our most cherished beliefs. And if we can in some way show how they *can* be simply *true*, then we will have gone far on the road to justification of our talk of and faith in God. Ian T. Ramsey, whose theories of the sense and reference of religious talk were considered in chapter four, also had theories of the justification of religious talk in terms of its truth. It is to his account of the ways in which talk of God can be judged "true" or "not true" that we now turn.

Ian T. Ramsey

As noted in the previous chapter, Ramsey thought that religious talk of God is best understood as qualified models. These have five uses or senses: to represent God, to evoke further disclosures, to indicate the logical status of God as distinct from but related to everyday talk, to generate stories and license discourse, and to refer to that which is encountered in a cosmic-disclosure situation. But we were left with an incomplete answer to the question "How do we know that it is God we are talking of?" Part of his answer was given, but a more complete answer remains. In terms of the choice of models for what is ultimate (theist or atheist) or for a set of models to represent the ultimate, Ramsey developed three sorts of criteria to be used to justify talk of God: rational or metaphysical, empirical, and "pragmatic."[31]

Simply, Ramsey's metaphysical justificatory criterion claimed that the more consistent, simple, comprehensive and coherent a family of theological models or a metaphysical "map" of the universe (whether theistic or atheistic) is, the better it is. If one is confronted with two or more opposing sets of ultimate claims (Catholic Christianity vs. Theravada Buddhism vs. secular atheism), these criteria can help one decide which is more likely to be true. By consistency, Ramsey intended to evaluate a system in terms of its ability to avoid category mistakes by breaking down its various logical regions into their properly separate places. In terms of religious language, Ramsey used this criterion in *Christian Discourse* "to see if we can separate out more reliable arguments from less reliable arguments in this tangled skein of theological discourse [i.e., atonement theology]."[32] By simplicity Ramsey claimed that the fewer key concepts or dominant models that a system had to make it hang together, the better it was. Much of Ramsey's explicitly theological work was intended to simplify Christian talk of God by clearly distinguishing the central from the peripheral. By comprehensiveness, Ramsey wanted nothing of importance left out. However, even a comprehensive history will exclude irrelevant events, and so a comprehensive picture or map of the world will exclude that which is irrelevant. Although it is difficult to specify this criterion precisely, a comprehensive book differs from a bare-bones essay and each has a different criterion of success; the criterion for a world view is more like the former. By coherence, Ramsey wanted to preclude those systems that have undiscovered contradictory elements. Any system that was self-contradictory—or, perhaps, lush with paradox—would rank low according to this criterion.

As a picture or view or map of the universe, Ramsey ranked theism highly: "Further, because of its relative simplicity and immense coherence and comprehensiveness, we can the more readily see why theism as a metaphysics has had the immense vogue and popularity it has had."[33] Interestingly, Ramsey omitted praising theism's consistency. The recurring bogus talk and linguistic confusions that have plagued Christian talk of God count against its consistency.

Ramsey's empirical justificatory criterion is not so straightforward. His discussion of his theory of empirical fit is more allusive than descriptive:

> The theological model works more like the fitting of a boot or shoe than like the "yes" or "no" of a roll call. In other words, we have a particular doctrine which, like a preferred and selected shoe, starts by appearing to meet our empirical needs. But on closer fitting to the phenomena the shoe may pinch. When tested against future slush or rain it may be proven to be not altogether watertight or it may be comfortable—yet it must not be too comfortable. In this way the test of a shoe is measured by its overall success in meeting a wide range of phenomena, by its overall success in meeting a variety of needs. Here is what I might call the method of empirical fit which is displayed by theological theorizing. . . .[34]

Another illustration Ramsey used to bring out the meaning of his criterion of empirical fit was to liken the theologian to "the archaeologist or anthropologist or detective who sees how his theory 'fits' a particular set of remains—though they may 'fit' many other theories, and at certain points fit ill with the one being sponsored."[35] The point here is that the theological model is to be justified somewhat differently than the scientific model. The former is better the more stable it is over a wide range of phenomena and the more fertile it is. The latter is better the more verifiable deductions that can be made from it and the more facts it brings to light. Yet both are never ultimate or final, for both can be improved or updated as new evidence, new ideas and new contexts demand.

Ramsey viewed justification of talk of God by empirical fit as an ongoing task. Although no model may be finally justified, some model may be so broadly based and so well-ensconced in an individual's or community's religious discourse that it is, for practical purposes, considered justified. One such model is the personal model for God, within the context of the ongoing Christian community, discussed in Ramseyan terms in the previous chapter. Yet even this model is subject to change as our understanding of what a person is changes. Ramsey's major criterion of the justification of religious language attempted to account for the life and death of models or symbols in concrete yet rational terms and thus became a hybrid containing a number of criteria, including the necessity of accounting for the facts of one's character as well as the facts of the world.[36]

The problem with Ramsey's notion of empirical fit is that it is vague. Once those models that positively do not fit the facts of the world are excluded (as 7B shoes are for 12D feet), a number of models and systems of models seem to fit the facts of the matter. What needs to be developed is a criterion that offers further choice among the models that, on grounds so far presented, can claim to be close to the truth. Ramsey's theory of the justification of talk of God includes both empirical and rational criteria. The weakness of these theories is that they are difficult to specify in any precise way. The strength of Ramsey's theories is that they present grounds that do not rely on a "fideist" position for their understanding and use, that do not assume that the falsificationist criterion of meaning is the final word, and that avoid suggesting that the world view of the theist is of a different order from the world view of the atheist.

But implicit in Ramsey's work is also a "pragmatic" criterion of truth. The response to a cosmic disclosure situation is most properly expressed in terms of a qualified model that captures not only the discernment one has in a situation of cosmic disclosure, but also the commitment that one takes up in that situation which is logically connected to the discernment. If this is accurate, then the commitment logically connected to the discernment can serve as a criterion for the justifiability of the discernment. And if the commitment is ultimate (which is true by definition if the disclosure is cosmic), then the commitment displayed by a person's life is a further criterion by which to judge his or her model for God.

But this criterion simply seems to make the evaluation even harder for it is a fact that some theists do appreciate that some humanistic atheists live, even on the theist's grounds, good lives (and vice versa)! This fact gives good grounds for Ramsey's claim that there may be similarities "which might not have been suspected between the theist's and the humanist's quest and attitude. . . ."[37] These similarities are not necessarily limited to vaguely similar commitments, e.g., an unselfish dedication to work to make this world a better place for all its inhabitants. Even though on first sight individuals' discernments may seem radically different, similarities may be discovered when open exploration is undertaken.[38] However, to discover how "friendly enemies" *significantly* agree and disagree is not an easy task—and may be one that is never completed and is one that is not guaranteed to lead to a successful outcome.

Nonetheless, some guidelines for such an evaluation can be found. If someone's commitment is evidently insincere, the discernment connected with it is suspect. Jonathan Edwards, the eighteenth-century American Puritan theologian, illustrated this:

> Thus it would be ridiculous for a man to plead that the commanding act of his will was to go to the public worship, while his feet carry him to a tavern or brothel house; or that the commanding act of his will was to give such a piece of money that he had in his hand, to a poor beggar while his hand at the same instant, kept it back, and held it fast.[39]

Similarly, it would be absurd for a believer to claim that God was infinitely gracious while he did not display his gratitude. It would be ridiculous for someone to claim that he believed in the liberation of all people while paying his employees a less-than-subsistence wage. In other words, negatively, the actions of a believer can show that his alleged ultimate claim is a false front. Positively, the performance of a believer, if, in the believer's view, it is congruent with his claim, displays what that claim means to a person who lives it.

Early in his career, Ramsey claimed that the pragmatic test "By their fruits you shall know them" is the most searching test.[40] Indeed, it seems that this *is* a test of truth, a pragmatic test that can be used to supplement the empirical and rational criteria discussed earlier. But what sort of life *is* worth living? This question is one of those "riddles of the sphinx" and in the end (but only in the *end*, not at the *beginning* of the testing of and justifying one's talk of God) it seems to be that one's commitment conquers; that in the end, one can only say *this* is the way I *must* live.

But while this may be the case, some further tests may be available. One wants to know not only the truth of one's talk of God, but also whether faith in God promotes a good and holy life—or whether other sorts of criteria count as well. To conclude this chapter on the justification of talk of God, one more theory will be considered, a theory that takes notes from Ramsey's works and specifies them in such a way as to overcome Ramsey's vagueness, and uses numerous other insights in recent empirical philosophy to outline how one may justify one's convictions—including, for many, the conviction one has that God does (not) exist. Southern Baptist theologian James W. McClendon, Jr., and secular atheist philosopher James M. Smith have coauthored a guide to the ways to understanding and justifying one's religious convictions. It is to their insights and oversights that we can now turn.

J. W. McClendon and J. M. Smith

Understanding Religious Convictions does not record a dialogue between the Christian and the atheist. Rather, it is a coauthored account of the elements in the process of attempting to understand and justify one's own or another's convictions. McClendon and Smith reject arguments that claim that reason —and reason alone—is a sufficient judge of the convictions of an individual or community, whether offered by theists or atheists.[41] Although they offer extensive arguments for this opposition, their basic problem with allowing reason alone to rule is that there is little agreement on just what argument, presumption or values are reasonable. In fact, it seems that what is reasonable is bound up with one's convictions—about what is reasonable!

But what are convictions? As McClendon and Smith use the term, a conviction is a "persistent belief such that if X (a person or a community) has a conviction, it will not easily be relinquished and it cannot be relinquished without making X a significantly different person (or community) than before."[42] Unlike Zuurdeeg, they do not define convictions topically. Convictions may be about anything. Unlike Phillips, they do not claim that convictions (in Phillips' Wittgensteinian terminology, certainties) are indubitable. Occasionally we do doubt even those beliefs that make us what we are. Unlike Hick, they are attempting to show in the concrete how, here and now, we can understand and justify our religious beliefs and how we can do so without assuming a single criterion of meaning and truth. As they note:

> But it may turn out, and should not *a priori* be excluded, that truth is not separable from other measures of value—from consistency, righteousness, justice, happiness, satisfaction. In that case we will be obliged to reckon with the interdependence of "ethical" or "aesthetic" with "epistemological" questions. The prospect that a concern for truth should not be isolable from a whole complex of other human goals and ideals should surprise no one. . . .[43]

While the truth of our convictions is important, their truth is not their *only* measure, although it may be essential.

What is necessary to express our convictions? Using the work of J. L. Austin (discussed in chapter three in conjunction with the work of Donald Evans), they discovered three necessary elements for a speech act, (1) primary, (2) representative and (3) affective or psychological. Assuming that a speaker and hearer can each speak and hear and that they share a language, (1) what the speaker says can be identified as a speech act—in the present case, it must be the speech act of *confession of convictions*; (2) the sentence the speaker utters must represent or relate to the facts—in the present case it must *represent* a state of affairs about which the speaker is convinced; (3) the speaker must have and display the appropriate *affect* of emotion for what he says—in the present case many affects are possible, but some such as "carelessness" will not do.[44] For instance, imagine the case of a person in the "pro-life" movement who is convinced (and so confesses), "Abortion of a human fetus is not therapy, but murder." Ordinarily, one will say this in response to a question, or proclaim it in a demonstration, or preach it at any who will listen. If this is indeed a persistent and formative belief, then the utterance is the expression of a conviction. This conviction is clearly about a state of affairs (abortion) and expresses a moral claim (its inherent wrongness). The attached emotion also seems necessary: Here, repugnance, disgust and sorrow each may be appropriate. But the absence of emotional or affective involvement ("Abortions are murder, but they don't bother me") suggests that the matter is not what it seems—either it is not a conviction, or the speaker is dissembling. To express our convictions properly all three elements—primary, representative and affective—are needed. The absence of any one of them indicates that something is wrong with what we say.

Why must we justify our convictions? "Justification is a response to challenges, and these challenges are both limited in number and definite in content."[45] In fact, what we regard as certainties—the beliefs upon which we would (and do?) stake our lives—are sometimes challenged. The various occasions in which challenges arise are what McClendon and Smith call the social matrices of justification. Here appears their most significant advance over other accounts of how convictional talk can be justified. Challenges are not freely floating in the air, but concrete, social, human occurrences that happen to persons. An anti-abortionist picketing an abortion clinic may be brought face-to-face with an unmarried and saddened thirteen-year-old mother-to-be who has no options left but abortion, whose carrying the baby to term would likely result in grave disability or death to the mother. This encounter between people who have differing convictions about a crucial matter is one of the social matrices of justification. Others include reformation, rebellion, revolution, the quest for truth and conversion.[46] In these situations, we *are* challenged to attempt to hold fast to our beliefs ("What would you do if you were in *my* shoes?") in the face of facts, values or seemingly reasonable beliefs that contradict our convictions. And if we don't respond to the challenge, can we still (reasonably) claim that our challenged belief is a conviction? "It would be as ridiculous . . ."—Jonathan Edwards' challenge fairly rings in our ears. Our convictions *are* challenged in a pluralistic world, be they about God or murder, and not to meet the challenges is to plead *nolo contendere*: to avoid the possibility of true meeting of other folk whether to vanquish them or to discover disguised similarities in position or to improve one's own beliefs. In the end, to refuse to attempt to understand and to justify one's most cherished beliefs in the face of challenges is to avoid part of human, social life.

But must we even have convictions? Logically, the answer is no. But if we have no convictions, what happens? The answer Christian McClendon and atheist Smith give is telling:

> To lack all persistent and central beliefs is, simply put, to lack character. Not just laudable or virtuous character, *but any character at all*. To be religious or sensual, ambitious or greedy, malicious or kind, radical or conservative, is (among other things) to have the sorts of beliefs we have called convictions. Lacking them, one may sporadically perform particular acts of kindness or cruelty, do conservative or radical things, act piously or irreverently, but these will be only reactions to particular circumstances, not expressions of settled or identifiable character. One is thus, in a way, the victim of these circumstances, just as a boat having freeboard but no sail or anchor is the victim of every chance wind. We grant that life can be led in this way, or, rather, that one can be led by life in this way. But if one still doubts whether such a life is satisfactory, let him consult Plato's *Republic* or *Gorgias*, where there are vivid portraits of *men who always do as they wish, yet never get what they want*. Nor is this merely an unfortunate but accidental fact about these men. For the man without convictions does not know what he wants in the settled way which would enable him to lead his life in a manner that might arrive at it.[47]

No, we don't need convictions to live; but we do need them to live happily.

To what criteria ought we appeal to justify our convictions? Simply, to whatever criteria are needed in the situation of challenge. "But if there is no logically necessary member of the list, and no single list which will satisfy all comers, we think it better to regard the possible terms of all such lists, not as criteria but as possible *loci* of justification."[48] The list includes truth, consistency, *eudaimonia*, satisfaction, righteousness, perhaps beauty, peace, love, justice, holiness and others. But even these *loci*, criteria or values are not neutral—for what each is in practice is convictional, as we noted in criticizing Basil Mitchell. It is the odd person who does not consider truth or consistency important, so it will appear on most lists; but there will be disagreements about how to discover the truth and what the proper criteria of truth are. Insofar as challenges are usually in terms of unmet criteria, the criteria of the challenges to which we respond will be the criteria or *loci* of justification.

In whose view do convictions need to be justified? This question is a bit tricky for the answer seems to be that a "justification must be effective in the eyes of the community, or the individual, holding the conviction. If it is *not* justified in their eyes, in what sense is it a justification at all?"[49] But if it is "in their eyes alone," are we in the same boat as D. Z. Phillips, in the end? In McClendon and Smith's view, the answer is no, for we are able to use insights even from those who do not share our "form of life" and "mode of discourse." Whereas in Phillips' view the various forms of life "just are" and cannot be justified or be "unjustified," in McClendon and Smith's view the very existence of plural (and competing) forms of life and modes of discourse is a social matrix that demands justification. The outcome of their "radically pluralist" position is summarized as follows:

> If I believe in God (am convinced of God) in a pluralistic world, a world in which I know there are men of good will who do not so believe, then my faith, if justified at all, must be a faith which takes account of that very pluralism which in part denies my faith. It must be faith justifiable (I must be

justified by my faith?) *in a world which includes unfaith*. Conversely, if I disbelieve, believe in no God, am convinced no God exists, in a world in which I know there are men who do so believe, then my conviction, if justified at all, must be one which takes account of that fact—it must be atheism *in a world which includes faith*. The pluralism which we envisage, then, does not obviate justification nor require narrowness of outlook, but it does require that the pluralism itself shall be internalized, so that it becomes a factor which my convictions take into account.[50]

While the eyes in which our convictions are to be justified are our eyes, those eyes must be able to see that there are other eyes, other visions, as sincere and honest as our own.

The concentration on the *situations* in which we utter our convictions, in which we are challenged, and in which we attempt to justify them, minimizes the dangers of subjectivism and fideism. Our faith expressed in our convictions was acquired socially; it must be expressed socially, and can be defended only in a social context. Our faith is not only a cognitive belief, but also an affective expression of our stance to the whole of life, a stance that involves the whole person. And it is the whole person (not his mind, soul or heart) that is challenged when his convictions are challenged.

Understanding Religious Convictions spends too much time disposing of rival interpreters of religious language and undermining supposed shortcuts to justifying convictions. Hence, the presentation of parts of the theory remains sketchy. Although the discussion of speech-acts and convictional speech-acts is detailed and complete, the theory of the justification of convictions and sets of convictions needs development. Only one *locus* of justification receives in-depth presentation (truth). The various social matrices in which justification arises are outlined, but not filled in. The contention that theology ought to serve as a "science of convictions" receives programmatic treatment, but no real defense. But just how theology is to do this in the face of the claim that there is no conviction-free ground on which to play the game of interconvictional justification remains unspecified. Throughout their provocative work remarkable insights occur and a neatly comprehensive theory of how to talk of God (or whatever one is convinced of) is developed. But, in the end, the reader wants to see just how these insights are to be applied in the concrete contexts of everyday life and strife. And to see that, further development of the themes present in this work is needed.[51]

Conclusion

The justification of talk of God is an ongoing task. In different ways, Mitchell, Phillips, Ramsey and especially McClendon and Smith have shown this. Mitchell has intimated that the task of justification is a real possibility. Just as one scientific paradigm has triumphed over or incorporated into itself other views, so the same may happen—in some instances—with talk of God. Phillips has shown that any attempt to explain away the phenomena of faith vitiates an honest portrayal of faith. We must begin with the believers' account of their faith and our account may not be totally at odds with or a reduction of the believers' account. Ramsey has shown that the truth matters. What we say of God is of major importance: but what we *say* is not ultimate for only God is. McClendon and Smith have developed these points in their own way. As they note, differences about convictional matters—be they about God or not—are "expected, but not inevitable, fundamental but not ultimate, and enduring but not inherently ineradicable."[52] To this ongoing task of justifying one's talk of God by understanding its sense, determining its reference and defending it against opponents—often ones who care for us deeply—this little book has been an invitation.

Notes

1. Ian Crombie, "Theology and Falsification," in *New Essays in Philosophical Theology*, ed. A. Flew and A. MacIntyre (London: SCM Press, 1955; New York: Macmillan, 1970).

2. John Hick, *Faith and Knowledge* (Glasgow: Collins, 1974), p. 169. This reprints the second edition (Ithaca: Cornell University Press,

1966) with a new preface. The discussion "Faith and Verification" expands an article, "Theology and Verification," *Theology Today* 17 (April 1960), which developed the position of the first edition of *Faith and Knowledge* (Ithaca: Cornell, 1957). In "Eschatological Verification Reconsidered," *Religious Studies* 13, 2 (June 1977): 189-202, Hick again clarifies his position in response to criticism, but remakes the same case he had made previously, which does not meet the objections discussed in the text.

3. Hick, *Faith and Knowledge*, p. 177. For an inspiring vision of one atheist's account of the world, see Bertrand Russell, "A Free Man's Worship" (1903) reprinted in *Why I Am Not a Christian* (London: Allen and Unwin; New York: Simon and Schuster, 1957).

4. Hick, *Faith and Knowledge*, p. 178.

5. *Ibid.*, p. 194.

6. *Ibid.*, p. 197.

7. *Ibid.*, p. vii.

8. *Ibid.*, p. viii; emphasis added.

9. *Ibid.*, p. 171.

10. *Ibid.*, pp. 181-86.

11. Basil Mitchell, *The Justification of Religious Belief* (London: Macmillan, 1973), chapters one and two.

12. *Ibid.*, pp. 39-40, citing Gilbert Ryle, "Induction and Hypothesis," *Proceedings of the Aristotelian Society*, Supplementary Volume, 1937.

13. *Ibid.*, p. 65, citing T. S. Kuhn, *The Structure of Scientific Revolutions*, 2nd ed. (enlarged), constituting volume II, number 2 of *Encyclopedia of Unified Science*, ed. Otto Neurath (Chicago: University of Chicago Press, 1970), p. 112.

14. *Ibid.*

15. *Ibid.*, p. 70, citing Kuhn, *op. cit.*, p. 149.

16. *Ibid.*, p. 95.

17. *Ibid.*, p. 134.

18. *Ibid.* For another approach to the comparison of science and religion see the works of Ian G. Barbour, especially his *Myths, Models and Paradigms* (New York: Harper and Row, 1974), where a rather different approach to the comparison of science and religion in the context of Kuhn's theories occurs.

19. D. Z. Phillips, *Religion Without Explanation* (Oxford: Basil Blackwell, 1976), p. 41.

20. *Ibid.*, p. 151; emphasis added.

21. Ludwig Wittgenstein, *On Certainty*, ed. G. E. M. Anscombe and G. H. von Wright; trans. Denis Paul and G. E. M. Anscombe (Oxford: Basil Blackwell, 1969; New York: Harper and Row [Torchbook], 1972).

22. Phillips, *Religion Without Explanation*, p. 164.

23. *Ibid.*, p. 168.

24. *Ibid.*, p. 181.

25. *Ibid.*

26. *Ibid.*

27. *Ibid.*, p. 189.

28. *Ibid.*, p. 188; emphasis added.

29. *Ibid.*, p. 100.

30. William James, *The Varieties of Religious Experience* (New York: Collier Books; London: Collier-Macmillan, 1961 [first published, 1902]), pp. 80, 115-59, 287, 378.

31. This discussion of Ramsey's theory of the justification of talk of God is expanded and amplified in my article "Ian Ramsey and Empirical Fit," *Journal of the American Academy of Religion* 45, 3 Supplement (September 1977).

32. Ian Ramsey, *Christian Discourse: Some Logical Explorations* (London: Oxford University Press, 1965), p. 29.

33. Ian Ramsey, unpublished typescript, untitled (apparently a draft for a projected major work, "Fact, Metaphysics and God") pp. B85/198f.

34. Ian Ramsey, *Models and Mystery* (London: Oxford University Press, 1964), p. 117.

35. Ian Ramsey, "Models and Mystery: Reply," *Theoria to Theory* 1, 3 (April 1967): 267.

36. This is developed more fully in "Ian Ramsey and Empirical Fit."

37. Ian Ramsey, *Models for Divine Activity*, ed. A. H. B. McClatchey (London: SCM Press, 1973), p. 64.

38. In fact, isn't this just what has happened (for better or worse) in the Christian-Marxist dialogue? See, for example, Roger Garaudy, "Communists and Christians in Dialogue," in *New Theology No. 5*, ed. M. Marty and D. Peerman (New York: Macmillan, 1968); also see G. Gutierrez, *A Theology of Liberation* (Maryknoll, N.Y.: Orbis Books, 1973), where a commitment to Christ is shown to be compatible with some aspects of Marxist thought. It should be noted, too, that it is hard to see how D. Z. Phillips would deal with this problem: In his view, the similarities would have to be incommensurable coincidences.

39. Jonathan Edwards, *A Treatise Concerning Religious Affections, in Three Parts* (1746); reprinted as *Religious Affections*, ed. John E. Smith, *The Works of Jonathan Edwards, II* (New Haven: Yale University Press, 1959), p. 426.

40. Ian Ramsey, "An Outline of A Christian Philosophy" (mimeographed, n.d. [probably, 1946]), p. 39.

41. James W. McClendon, Jr., and James M. Smith, *Understanding Religious Convictions* (Notre Dame: University of Notre Dame Press, 1975), chapter five.

42. *Ibid.*, p. 7.

43. *Ibid.*, p. 15.

44. Cf. *ibid.*, pp. 65-66. For present purposes, I have simplified the conditions laid out there.

45. *Ibid.*, p. 90.

46. *Ibid.*, pp. 171-83.

47. *Ibid.*, p. 111; emphasis added.

48. *Ibid.*, p. 163.

49. *Ibid.*, p. 182.

50. *Ibid.*, p. 183.

51. For further theological development of the "philosophy of religious language" developed in *Understanding Religious Convictions*, see McClendon, *Biography as Theology: How Life-Stories Can Remake Today's Theology* (Nashville: Abingdon Press, 1974).

52. McClendon and Smith, *Understanding Religious Convictions*, p. 7.

Afterword

In an introductory book like this one, suggestions for further reading usually appear. This book is no exception, but it should be noted that most of the suggestions I have for you are in the notes. Read the books I have talked about here—or at least those you have found interesting or intriguing. What follows is to be understood as only supplemental to the works cited in the notes.

Besides Antony Flew, the most important supporter for the sort of position discussed in chapter one is Kai Nielsen. In addition to the literature cited in notes, his *Scepticism* (New York: St. Martin's and London: Macmillan, 1973) is well done. For his approach to ethics, see his *Reason and Practice* (New York: Harper and Row, 1971) and *Ethics Without God* (London: Pemberton, 1973). Nielsen's strengths are the clarity of his understanding of the positions he opposes, the clarity of his writing, and his evolution in response to challenges. His weakness is that he seems (though he claims not to be) attached to a criterion of meaning indistinguishable from the principle of falsification.

Few today would accept the sort of criteria developed by the "non-cognitivist" theorists detailed in chapter two. Yet still claiming that he sticks to the positions he has developed, Paul van Buren has recently published *The Burden of Freedom: Americans and the God of Israel* (New York: Seabury Press, 1976). In discussing the mysteries of God's freedom, Israel's freedom, human freedom and Easter freedom, van Buren attempts to radically reunderstand Christianity's relation to Judaism. I think he throws out most (if not all) of what is distinctive about Christianity in an effort to get back to Christian roots in Judaism and to repudiate the traditional Christian claims about the Jews. This curious book exhibits at least part of the "cash-value" outcome of van Buren's philosophical position.

In recent years, the discussion of the Thomistic doctrines of

124

analogy has been rather important. Besides the books cited in the notes to chapter three, Patrick Sherry, "Analogy Today," *Philosophy* 51 (October 1976), offers an overview of the discussion. Two opposing views, Norris Clarke, S.J.'s and Kai Nielsen's, are presented in articles on analogy in the *Thomist* (January 1976). Finally, in a curiously mixed book that incorporates literary criticism, theology and philosophy, Brian Wicker attempts to show that any theory of metaphor needs the background of analogy. *The Story Shaped World: Fiction and Metaphysics: Some Variations on a Theme* (London: Athlone Press and Notre Dame: University of Notre Dame Press, 1975) is not easy to read, but it does contribute an interesting slant to a discussion that often tends to be rather dry. While in the past discussion of analogy has not been much informed by the empirical tradition in philosophy, perhaps the work of Burrell and Wicker augurs a new day. Finally, the works of Austin Farrer and E. L. Mascall, both Anglican Thomists, have also been written, informed by and in response to the empirical tradition. Farrer's *Faith and Speculation* (London: A. and C. Black, 1967), though difficult reading, shows a first-rate mind at work.

Donald Evans and D. Z. Phillips have continued to publish reflections based on their basic positions, some of which have been cited in the notes. While standing by the criticisms I have made of their positions in the text, I find them, nonetheless, two of the more interesting writers on the scene today. More will certainly be forthcoming from them and will be worth reading. Hopefully, Dallas High will be turning his mind to publication of further thoughts developing his work as well.

Any of the works of Ian Ramsey cited in the notes are worth reading on their own merits. There is still not an adequate presentation of his "whole" position. Donald Evans' excellent articles "Ian Ramsey on Talk About God," *Religious Studies* 7 (1971): 125-40, 213-26, are limited to Ramsey's understanding of talk of God and Jerry H. Gill's book, *Ian Ramsey: To Speak Responsibly of God* (London: Allen and Unwin, 1976) forces Ramsey's thought into a mold taken from the work of Michael Polanyi. In a similar vein, I should note that the work of John Hick, only a very small part of which has been discussed here, is worth reading. But, as with

Ramsey, it is well to run over the table of contents in Hick's books to see if the subjects treated are of interest.

But work on the philosophy of language is not confined only to the English-speaking realm of empiricism. Discussions of language are also numerous in the German and French philosophical traditions, and some translations, appropriations and explorations of these traditions are being made in English as well. The philosophical background is ably portrayed by Richard E. Palmer, *Hermeneutics: Interpretation Theory in Schleiermacher, Dilthey, Heidegger and Gadamer* (Evanston: Northwestern University Press, 1969). Generally, the works of Rudolf Bultmann, Ernst Fuchs and Gerhard Ebeling are of interest in this area. Gadamer's magnum opus, *Truth and Method*, trans. G. Barden and J. Cumming (New York: Seabury Press, 1975) is very difficult reading (and understanding!). A typical sort of approach made by theologians of this school is Gerhard Ebeling, *Introduction to a Theological Theory of Language*, trans. R. A. Wilson (London: Collins and Philadelphia: Fortress, 1973). Palmer's book contains an excellent bibliography of both philosophical and theological hermeneutics. To attempt to explore this very different approach to religious language would require another book besides the present one, so I shall leave the German scene with the above suggestions.

In a somewhat different vein—and one increasingly sympathetic to Anglo-American empiricism—Paul Ricoeur has incorporated insights from structuralism and phenomenology into an interesting hermeneutical theory. See his "Philosophical Hermeneutics and Theological Hermeneutics," *Studies in Religion/ Sciences Religieuses*, 5, 1 (1975): 14:33. Ricoeur's most recent major work is *Interpretation Theory: Discourse and the Surplus of Meaning* (Fort Worth: Texas Christian University Press, 1976). For appreciations of his work and a selected bibliography see *Paul Ricoeur and Biblical Hermeneutics*, ed. J. D. Crossan, *Semeia*, 4 (Scholars' Press, 1975). Ricoeur's work is beginning to have a major influence on the theological scene in this country, partly due to his teaching at the University of Chicago as well as in Paris.

The exploration of what it means to talk of God is far from completed. Explorers from many lands, with differing skills and backgrounds, with differing aims and interests, are investigating the problems of understanding talk of God. You are invited to join that exploration, to discover what you mean—as an individual who participates in a larger community—when you talk of God. You will have to meet challenges, you may change your mind and you might even enlarge your horizons. Although the exploration is difficult, and some would claim dangerous to faith, it is worthwhile. For may it not be the case that part of coming to know God is coming to be able to speak of him more clearly?

INDEX

cf. Christ; method and secret
of, 48–49
Justification, 64, 77–78, 88–90,
96–120, 127; loci of, 118, 119;
social matrices of, 116, 119

Klinefelter, Donald, 64
Kuhn, Thomas S., 101–102, 121

Language; cf. religious language;
game, 62–66, 73–75, 78, 118;
of imagery, 25; and life, 31;
limits of, 32; logic of, 69; and
world, 1
Le Vey, Anton, 54
Locke, John, 1
Locution; cf. Speech Act

Manuductio, 45, 84
Map, theological, 88, 110, 111
Marx, Karl, 52
Mascall, E.L., 125
McClendon, James Wm., 123;
and Smith, James M., 42, 93,
114–120, 122–123
Meaning, 11, 17, 29, 57, 68,
72–77, 96, 100, 115, 120; cf.
sense, reference, truth, "God"
Medical Professor, a, 78
"Meta-language," 69
Metaphor, 22, 61, 80, 81; cf.
model
Metaphysics, 9, 19, 103, 108–110
Michelangelo, 62
Miracles, 22–23
Mitchell, Basil, 100–104, 118, 120
Mode of discourse; cf. language
game
Models, 81–90, 110–112; cf.
analogy, Ramsey, I.T.,
metaphor
Moore, G.E., 1, 105–106, 109
Mythology, 29

Nielsen, Kai, 19–20, 62, 124, 125
Neutrality, 12–15, 57, 58, 61, 77

New Testament, 30, 48; cf. Bible
Non-cognitivism, 12–13, 21–42,
43, 50, 96
Nonsense, 6, 9, 31, 32, 76, 106,
108

Ogden, Schubert, 29
Old Testament, 47; cf. Bible
Onlook, 58–61

Palmer, Humphrey, 68
Palmer, Richard, 125
Paradigm, 101–104
Paradox, 111
Paul, Saint, 35–36
Performance, 75, 114
Performative, 56–57
Perlocution; cf. Speech Act
Perspective, 30, 32, 61–62, 101,
119–119
Phillips, D.Z., 42, 62–67, 70, 71,
72, 74–75, 94, 104–109, 115,
118, 120, 121–122, 125
Philosophy, 24, 74; empirical, 1, 3,
68, 126–127; tasks of, 62,
65–67, 106–107
Picture, 75; held us captive, 66;
religious beliefs as, 62–66
Platform image, 30–33, 37–38
Plato, 108, 117
Plausibility of theories, 100
Pluralism, 67, 91, 103, 117–119
Prayer, 30, 65, 66
Prescriptivism, 26–28
Presumption of atheism, 14, 77
Problem of Evil, 6–7, 18
Proofs of the existence of God,
22, 77, 100; cf. God
Prophecy, 21–24

Qualified models, 82–86, 88–90,
110

Ramsey, Ian T., 36, 79–95,
109–114, 120, 122, 125
Rapport, 59–60, 62

55008

DEMCO